Dear Marc

Thank you for the tunes!

In light

Lisa :) Sine

A Wolf Song

A Story of Forgiveness through Gratitude

Lisa Osina

Copyright © 2013 Lisa Osina.
Artwork © 2013 Susan K. Wagner

All rights reserved. No part of this book may be used or reproduced by any means, graphic, electronic, or mechanical, including photocopying, recording, taping or by any information storage retrieval system without the written permission of the publisher except in the case of brief quotations embodied in critical articles and reviews.

All artwork is the exclusive property of the artist, Susan K. Wagner. The artist withholds all rights, including but not limited to reproducing the work, using the work to make another work, distributing the work to the public, performing the work before the public and publicly displaying the work.

Author Credits:
Moving published 2000 by Internet Book Company

Balboa Press books may be ordered through booksellers or by contacting:

Balboa Press
A Division of Hay House
1663 Liberty Drive
Bloomington, IN 47403
www.balboapress.com
1 (877) 407-4847

Because of the dynamic nature of the Internet, any web addresses or links contained in this book may have changed since publication and may no longer be valid. The views expressed in this work are solely those of the author and do not necessarily reflect the views of the publisher, and the publisher hereby disclaims any responsibility for them.

The author of this book does not dispense medical advice or prescribe the use of any technique as a form of treatment for physical, emotional, or medical problems without the advice of a physician, either directly or indirectly. The intent of the author is only to offer information of a general nature to help you in your quest for emotional and spiritual well-being. In the event you use any of the information in this book for yourself, which is your constitutional right, the author and the publisher assume no responsibility for your actions.

Any people depicted in stock imagery provided by Thinkstock are models, and such images are being used for illustrative purposes only.
Certain stock imagery © Thinkstock.

ISBN: 978-1-4525-8590-1 (sc)
ISBN: 978-1-4525-8592-5 (hc)
ISBN: 978-1-4525-8591-8 (e)

Library of Congress Control Number: 2013919976

Printed in the United States of America.

Balboa Press rev. date: 11/8/2013

In Memory of

Arnold P. Sable Z"l
who wrote stories on his 1930's typewriter into
the night as I fell asleep as a child

Suzanne M. Kuzniar-Fogel Z"l
who inspired and pushed me to write A Wolf Song

I miss you

Introduction

A Wolf Song was conceived during a meditation on November 11, 2011 when a black wolf imparted the basic concepts of the story. Over the course of a year the wolf dictated each chapter to me. He only shared what he believed I needed to know and asked me to trust each weekend morning as I positioned myself in front of a blank screen. I had a routine. Outside my home, I would sit in my camper chair opposite my willows, in the dog's yard. Next door lived a family with two young children, a rescued donkey and two retired horses. I would close my eyes and my big black wolf with a white stripe down his nose, would appear in my imagination and proceed to download images, words and feelings about the next chapter. I would listen for the bird calls, hear their emotions and watch as the two kids played next door. Once full, I'd run indoors and type as quickly as I could before I forgot.

Once a few chapters were down, my mentors encouraged me to write an outline and I came up empty handed. I could not, for the life of me, set out where the story was going or how it would end. I only knew that Hanna and Margaret would meet up every ten years. My attempts to plan out the story only took me to an abyss. It was in the abyss of this unknown that I found the trust to just keep typing.

Over the course of the year, between 11/11/11 and 11/11/12, my friend Jane Keene became my 'reader' and each Sunday afternoon I would send off the next chapter or less and she would read it and send it back to me with comments. Thank you, Jane! Jane's immediate attention and feedback kept me engaged when sometimes I just wanted to go outside with the dogs and play ball!

I am an ordained minister of spirit with SHEs organization, a graduate of Lynn Andrews School of Sacred Arts and Training and a tax paraprofessional. I was born on the east coast of the United States, near Woodstock, N.Y. and in 1971, immigrated to Israel where my family remained. My multi-lingual background, coupled with a dyslexic thought and writing process, has produced a manuscript written with limited words and ideas that break barriers. You will experience backward sentences, paragraphs that take you forward when you're not quite ready, and moments of frustration when your 'inner-editor' kicks in. You will also find a deep compassion and love from the very first words. *A Wolf Song* will cradle you and then toss you to the sky. I promise, *A Wolf Song* will always be standing there, ready to catch you too.

From my heart to your heart, *A Wolf Song* is a healing story about tragedy, gratitude and forgiveness. When you read it, you will find mirrors that reflect your own life and use A Wolf Song as a template for recovery. There are very, very ancient concepts introduced such as embracing the unknown. The experiences in the story will show you how to apply them in this new world we live in.

May the loving force be with you.

Acknowledgements

It takes a village to publish a book. With great pleasure I'd like to express my gratitude to my blessed circle of supporters!

First and for most, to my husband, Ofer, who put up with hours of new age music streaming from the T.V. and me perched on the sofa, monopolizing the laptop, forgetful, and distracted. I thank you Simba and Cody, our four leggeds who would steal my mouse when they wanted to go out and play ball.

To my power animals, Nano, Nala, Big Black Wolf with White Stripe, Tiger, and Elephant, my opposite: You fill me, you guide me, and you are me. Blessed you's.

I want to thank Lynn Andrews and the Sisterhood of the Shields, who guided me to my power animals and continue to teach me every day. You make me want to be a better person now, then and forever. Your mirrors make each and every moment a lesson. Thank you for your continuance in my life!

Susan Wagner, Illustrator and Cover Artist, no words fulfill my gratitude for your courage, intuition and heart. Your ability to bring my sentences into a vision on paper exceeded all expectation. You have provided yet another layer to A Wolf Song and for that I thank you, dear sister.

Jane Keene, my 'reader', sister in circle and partner in this endeavor, your weekly review of each chapter hot off the screen, kept me going. My gift to you is to ensure that A Wolf Song is released to the light as we planned from the get go. My heart is full from you, Jane.

Catherine McSharry and Jane Keene of Sweetspot Video Productions, your production of my video for Kickstarter.com was an impeccable tool to raise the funds to birth A Wolf Song, I can't wait for my next opportunity to work with you! Sweet blessings to you and yours!

Virginia Morrel, of Balboa Press; you stalked me with monthly telephone calls for over a year! Bless you dear one, and thank you for your persistence which eventually led me to self-publish with Balboa!! Your support and confidence in A Wolf Song was monumental and I am so grateful to you, Megan, Janelle, Brandon and the rest of your wonderful team!

With a long drum roll, please acknowledge my village of angel backers! Michelle Gardner, Sandra Miller, Ken Conner, Thomas Cole, The O'Malley Family, The Levy Family, The Dikeman Family, Meghan Assenmacher, Feather Redfox, Cherie Price, Mary Alexander, Jane Sable-Friedman, Ajaib Bhadare, Pete Conder, The Lager Family, Dianne Reisen, Danielle Hess, Jane Keene. Your hard earned dollars have been handed over to my wonderful publisher, Balboa Press to produce the magical product that you have in your hands or on your screens. My gratitude list would not be complete without honorary mention of my mentors, Vicki Dobbs, Ann Vanino, Moss Rock Grinnell and Lyn Matthew who continue to witness and guide me.

Part I

Chapter 1

Two beasts from heaven were perched side by side on a crystal slab within this atmosphere. The air was like a vacuum. They stared into the beyond, peering through the veil of life, and watched earth from above. They were looking for bodies. These two souls—no ordinary ones—were on mapless journeys, and they needed the right fit. They were plodding, feeling, listening for a murmur or a calling to them. To be boys or girls, butterflies or simply swirls? Both had long journeys ahead of them, but they did not know their purpose, nor were they given the lessons. They only knew they would need sturdy bodies—bodies that would sustain a life in heaven and in hell.

These wolf spirits had enrolled with the Academy Mother Earth. This path would enhance their physical existence. Wolves are teachers, and these two particular wolf spirits were shattered from another time. On earth, in the physical, they would bring back the parts of their spirit that had fled home to the Pleiades in a past life. Now was the time for them to reemerge from the Pleiadian star of Maya, to be on earth and collect earthly wisdom.

One turned to the other. *Yup.* He nosed the other. *Strong bodies.* There was a physical consciousness between them; they felt fur and body parts, and they interacted physically in the ether, although once on earth, they would not be visible to the ordinary eye.

The wolves were transported telepathically to a ceremony of a pool of spirits and potential earth bodies. They were named here by their own animal spirits. Nano would be the male and Nala the female. So empty they were, so easy it was for them to choose. The spirit wolves walked instinctively toward their suited bodies, which appeared as pregnant mothers with translucent bellies about to give birth.

Nano chose a wealthy family, and Nala chose a poor one. What would happen to these two spirit wolves as they surrendered to the unknown earth bodies? Would they fully merge? They had chosen two girls, who would become women, who would experience the extremes of life. Yes, they would need sturdy bodies to endure the life ahead.

But after birth, once they had entered the physical, it would all be up to them, the two girls.

Nano and Nala stood as close as can be and nuzzled each other's ears, for soon they would separate. They heard a deep, penetrating tone; a chorus of voices engulfed them. The vibration of this sound surged through their spirit bodies and sent them through the ether into the form of the physical.

Waaaaaah. Nano's newborn heard screeching sounds and saw bright lights as he was being handled and bounced about. *Hmm, guess I'm here. This is going to be interesting.* He heard his own thought echo and felt the empty void.

Nano felt the loneliness of becoming physical; he could only hear his own voice. The outside noises made the inside silence even louder. So accustomed was he to hearing the voices of the all—the reverberations of earth and the universe, and now such a silence—such an *aloneness*. He heard his voice let out a wail, and everyone gathered around *her*. She was a girl! Nano knew that consciousness now belonged to her, the child. The warmth of their bodies filled her as Nano pulled back and allowed this spirit and body to be *hers*.

Oh, this is a good tool, this screaming, went through her. Was that a thought she heard? She was carried and washed and wrapped and then plopped on warmness. She felt a heartbeat and a cooing voice in her ear, a gentle touch on her new body. Warm, she knew she was physically feeling love, and she quieted. She was experiencing physical company for the first time; no chatter, just warm love. Then she slept on her mama's breast.

Meanwhile, Nala was being born, and Nano witnessed her birth along with his own birth. He saw her in the ether and around the body of the second newborn.

"I can go anywhere from here," Nala said. "I'm asleep, but I'm awake! Where the hell am I?"

Her kindred spirit, Nano, stayed firm and directed her. "Stay in her body now; get grounded. Get used to being there while she's asleep. Let her sleep."

"Waaaaaa!"

"Oh, she's screaming!" Nala cried.

"Yeah," Nano said. "She needs you inside her, close—now!"

Nano's girl, named Hanna, was more cooperative than Nala's, and her initial experiences, such as feeding time, were interesting. She ate the beauty through her eyes and began to grow and expand and get stronger inside. Outside, taking food into her mouth was clumsy and burpy, and she often lost most of what she took in. Hearing her body make demands seemed senseless to her spirit, though she learned quickly how essential these demands were in the physical. The mother's breast was soft, and it felt like an umbilical cord to the stars, which was where she yearned to be. Suckling was ecstasy for her spirit, and it also served the purpose of filling her belly, which seemed to growl endlessly.

The melting of body and spirit was quick, and she began to realize that there were thoughts going through her brain. Her spirit was imploding from within. She couldn't see the difference between herself and her wolf spirit, until eventually Hanna completely forgot about Nano.

Years one, two, and three of life on earth were a stew of trauma and battle, laughter and innocence. Although Hanna knew not of her wolf's existence anymore, she felt a deep connection with the pets living at home. There was Trixie, a king poodle. She stood tall, and she truly believed she was king of the house—yes, king. The cat, Lovely, stayed away from Trixie in front of the family, but at night they slept together. As Hanna watched the two, it brought back deep memories of howling, hunting, and hunger for a mate. She didn't understand where these memories came from; what she did know was that there was a friendship awaiting her, and this lonely girl was going to find it, she would search her entire city of Poughkeepsie, New York if she had to.

On family trips, Hanna would pass the time searching, looking with wonder into the eyes of each person she met. Her family was unaware of her search. She met many sets of dead eyes. It would make her stomach churn, and she would begin to count: two, four, six, eight. The numbers formed a wall of protection around her as she opened herself each time for friendship, and each time it was denied.

One day in that third-grade year, Hanna was searching at the park nearby her home after school. Could her friend be that little girl from the school yard who sat in the corner all alone and ate her sandwich one crumb at a time? Or was she the one who always followed the teacher around? She wondered. There was one girl in her class at school whom Hanna sometimes saw at the park, but she always seemed unapproachable. The girl had a twinkle in her eye that gave Hanna's belly a tug when their eyes occasionally met; it made Hanna want to cry with joy all of a sudden. *Could it be her?* she wondered. Her name was Margaret; she knew that from school. Hanna wondered if Margaret would be her special friend. She looked around the park and spotted her in the adjoining playground, near the swings. She thought, *I'll just see. Maybe she'll be nice. I could just go have a swing and see.*

"Hi, ya wanna play?" Hanna asked.

Margaret excitedly jumped up and pulled out her jump rope. The rope flew through the air, the wooden handle whacking Hanna in the mouth. Hanna fell backward, tasted blood in her mouth, and watched her front tooth fly out. She hit the ground hard and looked up as Margaret knelt down to her.

"Sorry," Margaret said, giving her a tissue to suck on.

"I have to find my tooth for the tooth fairy!" Hanna said. The girls searched the grass as the stream of blood from her mouth slowed and she regained her balance.

"Here it is!" Margaret grabbed the tooth from the ground and handed it to Hanna, who stuffed it in her pocket.

"Hi, I'm Hanna. Where do you live? We live on the hill."

"Do you know how to jump rope?" Margaret asked.

"Yeah, a little, I think."

Margaret started chanting a song that Hanna didn't know, but she knew the jump, so she skipped into Margaret's rope. They found themselves jumping in turn, same rope, facing each other, smiling brightly and breathing hard. They continued for a while, searching in each other's eyes. As their gazes locked into each other, both began to hear a choir of voices from within, and both began to sing the same tune. Hanna sang the words:

> Oh, softly I touch.
> You and I, how softly we know
> That the sound of our voice will
> Let our spirits show.

Margaret began to howl, and still the two girls jumped on.

When they had tired and flopped down on some grass nearby, Margaret held tight to the jump rope, as if it held the song in its coils. She wrapped the rope around her, caressed it, sucked on it, and chewed it. Hanna was close to sleep when Margaret kneed her in the side. "Did you hear that song?" she asked.

Hanna sat up, leaning back on her hands. She looked up to the sky and felt like howling again. She turned to Margaret. "It made me feel like a wolf!"

"And me! I felt like a wolf in the snow or something, like I could be anything. What were the words again?"

"'The sound of our voice will let our spirits show.' And Margaret, you howled! You heard it too, didn't you? You heard the voice. I know you did!" Hanna seemed frightened.

"I heard, Hanna. I heard the words you sang. It was many, many voices singing, and many wolves singing with them!"

"This is just like in a book or a movie," Hanna said. "If I told anyone about this, they wouldn't believe me. They would say I'm daydreaming again, making up things, but you, Margaret, you heard it too, so we know we're not making it up, right? It's not making believe, right? Here, let's try it again. Let's see if it happens again. What were we doing?"

Margaret stood up with her jump rope and started to jump a two-step skip. Hanna warmed up for a moment and then jumped in. They synced into a simultaneous rhythm with their skips and quickly lost themselves in the movement.

Nala and Nano sat side by side in the tree above. They watched the motion the girls were making and gave each other a nose-to-nose rub; they breathed into each other's face and neck and felt their spirit breaths.

"Nice to see you," said one. "If we keep them jumping, we can visit with each other, make them love what they are doing."

"Give her the song again; she loves it," said the other.

"Yeah, I'll give her the tone; you only gave yours a howl. Let her sing."

"Grrrrrrrr... she needs to howl."

"Connect her with us. She can't just howl all the time. The others will think she's crazy! Give her the tone!"

"Grrrrrrr," Nala growled.

The girls were jumping, one howling, the other trying to remember the song.

"Come on, Margaret! You remember the song. Let's try and sing it again! 'Oh, softly I touch...'"

Margaret opened her mouth, and all that came out was a long, lonely howl. Her face cracked at the sound, and she stopped jumping midstream. Hanna tripped on the rope, and they both fell to the ground.

"There, you see what you did?" Nano said to Nala. "She needs the tone; she needs the song! Give it to her!"

"Nope," Nala responded. "Keep her wild. She'll have to learn it later. Let her fall and trip on it for now. Your girl knows it; she can sing it to her."

"But then they won't create the tone that calls us." Nano nosed her in the ribs, and Nala jumped from her lazy stance.

Nano continued, "We have to get them ready for later... so they know how to call us."

Hanna's wolf spirit, Nano, was well beyond a size imaginable. All black he was, with a white stripe down his bushy tail—like a skunk. His triangular face had a white stripe between his eyes, reaching to the top of his head. He started circling Nala and nosing her, butting her in her butt and moving her into a circular movement. The two began to intertwine in a spiral motion, their furs combining, their noses sniffing their tails, footprints forming a spiral of markings at their feet, soft puffs of their spirit forming a path underneath them.

The girls recovered from their fall. They lay side by side on the grass and looked into the sky full of clouds and streaming sunshine.

"What do you see up there in the sky, Margaret?" Hanna asked. "Don't those clouds look like things to you? I see sheep all the time; they follow each other, like we do in the cafeteria at lunchtime."

"I see carnivals and fun places to jump and play," Margaret answered as she turned over to her side and laid her head on the soft grass.

"Can you imagine being this small?" she asked as she looked through the grass at ground level.

"I imagine that each blade of grass is a huge tree towering above me!" Margaret jumped up in excitement and began hopping over the grass, reaching to the sky.

"What is that, that we imagine, Hanna? Why can't we touch it with our finger? I can see it in my imagination, all those things, but I can't touch them... they get lost..." Margaret lamented. She stared down at Hanna with her hand on her hip, waiting for her to respond.

Hanna sat up. She'd been listening to Margaret and wondering what this word *imnation* was and what it had to do with sheep and grass, and how she could ever be so small that grass towered over her.

"Margaret, I don't understand you. What's this word, *imnation*?"

Margaret laughed. "You mean *ima-gin-a-tion*. It's the stories that you have in your eyes, the things we make up, the way we make believe; that comes from imagination. Mommy always says, she always says, if we feel sad or angry, we should imagine ourselves in a world of clouds like cotton candy, pink and blue and sweet. Make our whole body feel sweet and soft and whole. Big lollipops and cotton candy, she always says. Imagine that."

"Oh, that," Hanna said. Her head was bowed; she stared at her hands as they played with a piece of grass. "I'm not allowed. It's like make-believe, and it's against our house rules."

"Oh come on, Hanna." Margaret pushed her arm. "You don't have to obey house rules here, you know that! You can imagine anything here with me on the grass; with our wolves, we can!"

Hanna lay back on the grass again. She tried to open her heart to the fun of imagining. It happened like magic the moment she gave herself permission, and within no time, she had soared high into the sky above, where she found a cloud. It was pink, purple, and golden yellow, with a deep red bottom, and she curled up in the center, sensing the boundaries and feeling safe there. Here, her worries disappeared, and her questions dissolved. She lay there for quite a while, just experiencing the make-believe. *It is so real*, she thought.

Then suddenly her vision changed. At first she couldn't believe her eyes. A shiver went through her, chilling her all over, but she so taken by her vision that she dared not move. Shadows appeared as the sun shone through clouds above onto her cloud. A darker backdrop appeared, and she saw a giant wolf head before her... it was black, and she knew it was male. A striking white stripe split the wolf in half, and she saw him transform from male to female before her eyes. The female invited her, and she felt herself draw up close to the dark, long, silky fur. She buried her face in her side, and the feminine aspect of Nano gave her a lick.

Then Hanna stood in her vision and saw the other side, the male, the tall and postured; he had such a stare, and she felt him penetrate her with his look. It felt warm inside, and she welcomed it, instinctually knowing that it was food for her spirit. He pointed his nose to the sky and howled, and Hanna quickly drew back from him as he circled her. He beckoned her to him, and she was able to stand next to him. They stood side by side, nose to nose; the wolf reared up in the air and told her to mount. She complied, and they lifted off together into the sky toward the stars. Hanna looked down at her world and up at the unknown to her imagination. She wasn't sure what was "real" and what wasn't or if Margaret were still on the grass. These thoughts brought her back to earth with a jolt, and she felt she had hit the ground as she came out of her dream.

"Wow, Margaret, we're still here! Did you see any of that?" Hanna asked, standing up and walking over to Margaret, who was playing on the swing nearby. "Were you imagining as well?" Hanna asked.

Margaret laughed. "No, Hanna. I was watching you."

"What did I look like? Was I moving with my body? Did you see the wolf?"

Margaret laughed again and gently jumped off her swing in midflight. "You saw a wolf? I see wolves too! No, you looked like you were sleeping, and you were smiling."

Hanna sighed in relief. "Oh, that's good. So we can do this anytime? Just go off?" Hanna continued questioning Margaret about this new imagination thing; it *was* a thing to her. Like a new toy, she reveled at this new place she could go.

Margaret wondered if Hanna knew the rules, like how to come back gently and what to do if bad things happened. *Ah, she'll learn just like I did*, she thought, *I better not tell her. She'll find out.*

Margaret's mother, Joan, would take the path from the apartment to the playground each afternoon to meet her daughter. She would start calling when she reached voice range, always hoping that Margaret would shorten her walk and meet her halfway. Margaret could hear her calling, and Hanna looked up when she heard it too.

"Suppose we gotta go home now," Hanna said, her eyes shifting to the ground before looking up. "Margaret, can we meet every day from now on for the rest of our lives? Can we? Can we? We can go on journeys together. If you tell me where you are going, I can follow with my imagination. I know it!"

Margaret was distracted with the sound of her mom. She gave Hanna a quick hug and said, "See you again soon," and ran off.

Hanna was left on the grass to watch Margaret run into the distance. *I hope she comes back, I sure hope she comes back*, she thought. *Maybe I'll just wait here.* Hanna jumped on the swing and reflected on her dream with the wolf, his enormous size still resonating inside her. After a while, Hanna's brother Michal came to fetch her home.

The brook they called Salkill Creek flowed all the way from the school clear across town, passing by the rec field and the cemetery, then twisting straight through town and going under Turnpike Bridge to head down to the Walkill River. Margaret liked to follow the water, as it led directly to her house and she didn't have to talk to anyone on the way home. She loved the time alone; it was precious. At home, it was always so busy and noisy. Her mother always had people over, and Margaret sometimes wished she lived like Rapunzel, up in a tower where she could have some peace and quiet. Today, the water rushed quickly by as she walked; it was spring, and the creek was high. She often wondered what it would be like to be a leaf traveling on top of the brook. Where would it end up? Would it survive the current?

Margaret often wondered how she survived the current of her life, and now her insides were all mixed up after meeting Hanna. She had felt and seen things like never before, and she knew that things just wouldn't be the same again. In fact, other things seemed different too: her perception was keener, colors were brighter, and the sound of the birds seemed more a chorus of angels. *All alive is me, and all alive is all*, she found herself thinking. Overwhelmed, she heard her mother calling again and quickly ran toward her.

Hanna followed Michal, looking intent on every step forward she took… *One, two, three, four, five, count the steps. How many steps to home? 347. Six, seven, eight…*

"Had a good day today, Hanny? We did. Had a ripping kickball match in the gym this morning. I scored seven points!"

Nine, ten, eleven, twelve… why does he always try and mix me up by talking? she thought and continued counting her steps all the way home, looking nowhere but down. She trusted the sound of her brother's footsteps as she eventually reached 340, 341, 342. *Ah, must be getting close*, she thought and raised her head up toward her home—not that she was sure she'd be safe there, but that was a different matter.

"So, ya made it again? Survived the evil forest?" Michal teased.

Hanna looked up, happy and able to talk. "Michal, I know about the monsters under your bed; I hear you make deals with them every night!"

They ran up the porch steps and piled into the house, down the hallway to the big kitchen in the back of the house, where they always sat around the table after school to wait for their milk and cookies.

A few years back, Hanna had run into a wolf in the front yard, and since then, her walk home was full of fear that the wolf would come back and devour her. Sitting in the safe kitchen, waiting for Ma's cookies, Hanna thought about the wolf she'd met in the yard and the one she dreamed about in the playground. Her body became shivery as she realized they were one. Tears appeared. She felt choked up as she realized that she had met this wolf before. She also knew that she was safe from this wolf and would never have to count again on the way home.

As Margaret and Joan approached the ivy- and jasmine-clad porch of their apartment, the scent hit her nostrils; the smell of home soothed her. *It must be cleaning day. I have chores to do!* Margaret remembered.

"Mum, I met a new friend. Her name is Hanna, and she can jump rope too!"

"Yes," Joan responded, tight-lipped, hand on her hip.

"I know I have chores. I'm dust mopping today. I looked this morning."

Joan smiled and gave her a pat on the back and a kiss on her head as she came up the porch steps. "Thata girl!"

Margaret ran into the house and headed for the laundry room to get the dust mop. She didn't mind dust mopping. It gave her a feeling of cleaning and clearing, and she felt satisfied when she saw all the dust she'd collected. Once her chores were finished, she too sat at the kitchen table for her snack, and Joan joined her with a plate of warm cookies.

Margaret continued telling her about her new friend. "So, Mum, I'm going to stop at the park every day after school to jump rope with my new friend, Hanna, okay?"

Finally, Joan thought, *Margaret has a friend*. It filled her with joy, and Joan knew that she could start planning her daughter's birthday party, now that there was someone to invite. *I have such a solitary daughter.*

Hanna was well ready for her mother to bring out the cookie jar, which she kept up on the highest shelf of the kitchen, out of sight, out of reach. A good cookie steal was not easy in their house. Cookies were such a treat, always home-baked by Mom. Hanna and her brother would sit and guess which kind their mom was baking by strong aromas that filled the house. Today, it was sugar cookies, with nuts and cinnamon, one of Hanna's favorites. Her mom poured the milk.

"Mom, I made a new friend today. Her name is Margaret, and she had a jump rope, and we jumped rope, and we sang together, and we lay in the grass today in the park. Mom, can I have a jump rope? I can jump rope, Mom; did ya know?"

"Where does Margaret live, Hanna?"

"Down the hill, Mom. I saw her going toward the woods when she went home. Maybe down near the railroad station, down by the river?"

"There's no houses down there, except for the apartment complex," her mom said thoughtfully. "Hmm, you'll have to ask her next time. Maybe you can walk home together."

"I don't think so, Mom. It wasn't near our house at all. But I'll see her tomorrow after school in the park." Hanna suddenly realized that she didn't really know anything about Margaret, only that she jumped rope, and when they did it together, something happened between them. She knew she couldn't tell her mom about it; she didn't really know what to tell her about it.

"So, Mom, can I have a jump rope?" Hanna finished up her cookies, slurped up the rest of the milk, and jumped off the chair to the linoleum floor, straight onto the two black squares in front (not to touch the white ones!) and hopscotched across the kitchen floor.

"I'm going to find a rope!" she told her mom and ran out of the house through the backdoor into the backyard.

Hanna's yard was a salad of landscapes. In front, near the house, there was soft green grass and her mom's flower beds and herbs. At the end of the grass toward the back, there was a fruit orchard of apple and pear trees, where Hanna often played under the branches. Today Hanna was concentrating on the junk piles, hoping to find a rope to practice with. The piles were in the far corner of the yard behind the orchard. Mom had warned her of snakes there, so Hanna was very careful and alert, hoping to find something with a rope on it.

She suddenly noticed a mouse, and then a bird perched on a lower fence. She heard the rush of leaves and could almost feel a snake skim by her. She jumped in surprise but realized the mouse and the bird sat in place watching. They hadn't moved an inch! *How's that?* she thought. *Didn't they see the snake? Or feel it?* Hanna was confused and very slowly approached the bird so as not to startle it. Hanna got so close to the bird, she was nearly nose to beak with it when she started hearing bells and chimes in her head. She closed her eyes for a second and saw Margaret's face in the bird. Margaret smiled at her, and their eyes met. A symphony erupted in Hanna's head, and she swayed to the music and smiled blissfully, totally forgetting about her search for the rope.

Hanna had never seen such things before. The vision and the music overwhelmed her and abruptly brought her back to the orchard and to her backyard. Her mom, Carol, was calling, and Michal was standing in front of her.

"What were you doing?" he asked.

Hanna looked at him and felt the distance between where she just was and where she was now.

"Oh, nothing, Michal. I was looking at this bird. I was trying to be quiet and still so it wouldn't move."

"What bird?" he asked.

"The one right here on the…" Hanna looked over, and the bird—there was no bird.

"It must have flown off," Hanna said, wondering if it was ever there at all.

"Come on, Michal. Help me find a rope. Do you know how to jump rope? Did you see that girl I met today? She can jump rope!"

"I know where there's a rope—in the garage. We have one in the trunk of the car, but it's a big rope; let's go see," he said, running back toward the house, where the garage stood.

Hanna trailed slowly behind. She felt like she was floating as she walked through the orchard and onto the soft green grass. A sudden urge to lie down came over her, and she found a comfy spot on the grass. Hanna fell to asleep instantly; her dreams took her back to the bird, the music, and Margaret.

"Margaret, what are you doing?" Joan asked as she put her head around the bedroom door.

Margaret had disappeared for a while and lay down for a nap as she, too, felt a sudden exhaustion, like there were magnets on her all pulling her to lie down and close her eyes. She found herself in her dreams, but it was different. She was awake, and Hanna was with her and they were in a field full of animals and butterflies and birds. She could hear the music of the birdsongs, and bees buzzing sounded like a symphony of violins. Amazed by the beauty, the light, and the sound, Margaret searched her surroundings. Hanna sat next to her; she too was amazed and in awe of what they were experiencing. Neither could talk; they just looked at each other, jaws dropped, eyes peeled, cheeks taut. Tears ran down both their faces, and yet there were no sobs or thoughts of grief. Each wept tears of joy and amazement, exuding unprecedented joy.

"*Margaret!*"

"Yeah, Mum," she responded from underneath her dream, wondering if she could hear her. She lifted her head for a moment and looked toward the door. "I'm napping, Mom. I'll be down in a while."

Joan came into the room and stood over her bed. "What are you up to, Margaret? You don't look asleep."

"I'm daydreaming, I think. You remember I told you that I met a new friend today, Mum? Her name is Hanna, she lives on the hill. I was daydreaming about her just now, and she was soooo real! How can that be, Mum?"

"Oh, there you go again, letting your imagination take over. Margaret, we've discussed this. You know what is real is when your eyes are open. The make-believe comes when you close them."

"But, Mum, it seems more real in my dreams!" Margaret argued and felt deep inside that this was true. *Mum just doesn't know*, she thought.

Under a full moon and clear sky, the two wolves barked and howled. The air was brisk, winter was coming, and their fur had thickened; tufts of white and black fur stuck out of both. They were tousled and aroused; they'd been wrestling in the wind, and their coats were rough and disheveled. They were breathless and eventually fell to rest one on top of the other, their legs intertwining. "Ah, that was a blast! The air, the wind, I feel that call of winter!" one said.

The other noted, "The girls have met. This is good. We celebrate their union; we celebrate the journey before them!"

The two circled each other, nose to tail, nose to tail. Their bodies turned into a swirling spiral of black and white light and rose above the hilltop where they had stood. They harmonized in their wolf song and let their spirits flow and merge momentarily and then separate into two spirals—one white, one black—and they fell back into their ether bodies on the hilltop.

"The girls have many journeys to travel. We will stay with them always, and they will need our help," one said.

"Yes." The other nodded and replied, "We will teach them our wolf song, one verse at a time. We will circle around each year and teach them the song. That's what we'll do. Grrrrrr, yes, hmmmmm, grrrrr, that's what we'll do."

> Oh, softly I touch.
> You and I, how softly we know
> That the sound of our voice will
> Let our spirits show.

Hanna lay in her bed that night looking out at the stars. She loved her cozy bed; it was here she would dream about life and wonder what life was. It was here that Mommy read to her and she was safe. Here she didn't have to count anything, and it was here she could be anywhere, with no cracks to step on. She thought of Margaret and the song they had sung. She felt the words touching her: "that the sound of our voice will let our spirits show." "Ahhhhhhhh," she sang softly in a high chord. As she let out the air and let it funnel through her vocal chords, she felt her throat vibrate and the wind of sound come from her.

"Ahhhhhhhhh," she continued. "Ahhhhhhhhhhh." *It feels so good!* she thought and continued to let her spirit sound out of her bedroom window to the black, star-studded sky.

Way above, she saw a swirl of stars; the lights delighted her as she watched the spiral flirting with the light. The more she focused on it, the more she seemed to see the spiral form two colors—black and white. She saw the black as blue sparkles against the dark sky, and then even more… she stared and felt a tug in her belly, and then she knew that she was watching two bodies circling round each other. The wolves revealed themselves for seconds and whooshed out of sight.

Carol was calling, and Hanna quieted her toning and called back, "I'm just practicing my voice, Mom, for music class at school. We're learning the scales."

"Okay, darling. Don't be too loud now; your brother is sleeping."

"Okay, Mom," she called back and settled back down into her fluffy white blanket. She fell asleep as her head hit the pillow.

"Hanna, get up this moment! Why are you sleeping? Are you sick? It's only six o'clock, and we haven't even eaten dinner. Why aren't you doing something? Don't you have homework? Hanna?"

Hanna could hear his voice. Feelings of sheer pleasure and dread ran through her. She squirmed in her bed, not sure how to react, rubbing her face in her pillow and digging even further into her blanket.

"Hi, Dad," she managed to blurt. He was towering over her bed, his hands on his hips. Then he reached for her blanket and flipped it up in the air, throwing Hanna sideways and over the other side of the bed. She quickly stood up and scowled.

"Dad, I was resting! I didn't have any homework. Mom let me! What's for dinner tonight? I'm starving."

Hanna saw his face soften. Jay thought of the special meal he'd planned on the way home from the office, and he was eager to share it with his family. He kept a tight house. His wife, Carol, stayed at home with the house and the kids, but her cooking left the family hungry too many times, so Jay had taken over cooking duties, adding on to his sixty-hour week at his law firm. The cooking fulfilled him somehow, and he loved his own dishes. "I'm making stuffed pork roast tonight, lovey. Picked up some mean ones at the butcher today. You want to come down and help me?"

Hanna savored the moments she spent with her dad when he was cooking. He felt so good, and he would laugh and make jokes. His face would show happy lines around his eyes and chin. She loved drawing his happy lines during class at school; it always brought her closer to him. Dad loved cooking, and Dad hated working. Hanna never understood why he was at work so much when he hated it. She would see him in the morning, but he had his work face on. That meant *do not approach*, and if she did, he would shoo her away and look at her with the most awful face. A lump would form in Hanna's throat each time she saw that face.

But today he was happy and cooking, and Hanna jumped out of bed at the chance to have some good time with Da.

"Yaaaay, Dad," she shouted, and wrapped her arms round him, her face smushing into his soft comforting stomach. Dad always smelled of something that was in the bathroom; she was still testing which bottle it came from. Hanna loved smells.

"Dad, can I try on that stuff you wear? I want to smell like you!"

"Hanna, that's for men. You should ask Mommy to try her perfume—you'll like it better."

"Dad, I want to make a smell that smells like the grass and the trees! Wouldn't that be fun, Dad, to smell of grass?"

"Hanna, sometimes I wonder about you," he said. Her heart dropped as he showed his disapproval. It didn't really matter about the grass or the smell—she didn't really mean it—but now he was mad at her.

She grabbed his hand. "Dad," she said as she gazed into his eyes with her most loving look. "Dad, show me your pork roast!"

He smiled at her lovingly, and Hanna took it and healed her hurt from his remark. She felt better and ran down the stairs ahead of him into the kitchen and peered into the shopping bags on the kitchen table. "Can I help make the stuffing for the pork roast? Dad, I remember how you do it. Do we have those breadcrumbs you used?"

"Yeah, they are up on the top shelf; I'll grab them for you. Why don't you set yourself up at the counter next to the sink? Get the stool from the dining room so you'll reach."

Hanna celebrated him allowing her to help. Most times he was grumpy when he started cooking and didn't want her around. *He always gets happy in the kitchen,* she thought, *no matter what mood he's in when he comes home. By the time dinner's ready, Dad always has a smile on his face.*

Hanna paid attention to faces so much at home. She never knew who was going to flip out on her or degrade her or just say awful things. She learned to be careful at home and to watch and listen when they weren't looking. Her mom and dad talked together sometimes at night; they talked about war and death and bankruptcy and other words she didn't know. She didn't understand why they were making up these horrible stories, and when she asked, her mother would say, "It's nothing to do with you, darling; don't worry yourself."

As she mixed up the ingredients for the stuffing, Hanna was careful to work slowly and methodically, like her dad taught her; otherwise, he would be mad and take it all away. Or he would wag his finger if something spilled, and yell at her, "Or else!" Then he would glare at her. For Hanna, this was the worst. When he said *or else.* Or else what? She scowled, her frown beating into the stuffing mix; she almost sent some of it flying out of the bowl. All worked up, Hanna put the spoon down in the bowl and looked out the window into her mother's flower beds. So beautiful, they always made her feel better. She stared and tried to breathe deeply.

"Oh, Hanna, how's my baby girl today?" Jay hugged her as she stood on the chair. Hanna relaxed back into his embrace.

"I met a new friend today, Dad. Her name is Margaret, and her jump rope hit me in the mouth and knocked out my tooth."

Hanna dug her hand in her pocket and pulled out the tooth, reaching out to him. "See?"

Jay was pulling the pork roast out of the fridge.

"Yes, Hanna. You'll have to put it under your pillow tonight for the tooth fairy."

He neglected to look at the tooth, and Hanna took note. She put it back in her pocket.

"Okay, Dad. I'm done. How are you going to stuff this into the pork?"

Jay rolled out the meat and showed Hanna how to spread the stuffing on the flat strip of meat. Then he rolled the meat and stuffing into a log and then wrapped it with string. The oven was hot, and Jay put the roasting tin inside and shut the door. Hanna watched him intensely. Every movement he made drew her in. She watched for signs of frustration; she enjoyed his grace this time and felt a love she didn't know how to hold.

"Dad, I'm going out to find that rope Michal found for me. Will you jump rope with me while dinner is cooking?"

"Hanna, jump roping is for girls your age. I can't jump rope with you."

"Yes, you can, Dad. I'll show you. It's so much fun!"

Hanna ran outside feeling like she was escaping his spell. She loved him so and knew she wasn't always loved by him. She never knew how to behave with him. She thought, *maybe if he jumps rope with me, he'll see the wolves. Maybe he'll hear the song.*

Chapter 2

In the months that followed, Margaret and Hanna met up most every day after school in the park. They honed their jump-roping skills, but mostly they lay in the grass and talked. They were both nine years old already and had so much to catch up on.

Hanna spent hours telling Margaret about her house. She described her home room by room, the closets and window bays included. She told her about her chores and about the place in the back of the yard where she saw the bird appear and then the vision. She talked about her dad a lot. The love/dread feelings she had for him confused her, and she didn't understand why Michal was oblivious. She was glad Margaret would listen.

Margaret didn't have a father and was hungry for Hanna's stories about her dad, even when she cried after he'd been mean to her. Hanna would tell Margaret how lucky she was not to have a man in the house. Margaret asked for every detail, visualizing it in her head, but she could not imagine the feeling. There were no men where she lived. Her dad was *long gone*, at least that's what Mom told her.

One day, like any other day, the two were rolling down the grassy hill in back of the swings. At the bottom, they tumbled into each other and landed laughing and squealing with excitement.

"Hanna, my mom is planning a big birthday party for me. I have all the invitations in my book bag. Will you come with me to deliver them?

"Margaret, my birthday's next week too! My Da said he'd take me horseback riding in the country. They have trails there that we always pass on the way to Montgomery Ward, and he finally said we could go. What day is your birthday?"

"September 23, Tuesday. You can come to my party, right?"

"What? Margaret! I don't believe it—we're twins! My birthday is September 23 too!"

"What? We're twins? Wow!" Margaret was flabbergasted. She turned to Hanna, frowning. "That's crazy!"

Hanna jumped up and ran around in a big circle with her hands outstretched, feeling the wind against her. The warm air enveloped her as she ran. Her smile was so wide as she sang out loud:

> Oh, softly I touch.
> You and I, how softly we know
> That the sound of our voice will
> Let our spirits show.

"Margaret, get up and come sing with me! I feel like we could fly! We're *twins*!"

The wolves were watching. "Grrrrrr, it is so."

"Mmmmmmrrrrrr, it is. Yeah, I feel us melding. Yeah, it's good, those two, it's good. They know now. They are each other; they are separate, but they are each other. Ahhhhh, yes, I sense this is good, but maybe not. They need an ally. I see this coming. They need a wise one, an elder to go to. We are not welcome in their world. They need an ally to go to. I'll send Hanna a grandmother type woman to live near her."

"What will you send Margaret?"

"I will send her a furry dog, a puppy, someone she can chase and care for."

"How will it assist Margaret?"

"She will learn how to howl good. She will get wolf wisdom. She will hunt and guard."

Nano began to circle Nala. He nudged her with his nose; he butted her gently in her torso. She nodded to him.

"You feel I should give Margaret more tools of the earth, like you do for Hanna? You give her the words to the song; I give Margaret the sound of the words. You give her a human to explain. I give her the mirror of the human, her four legs. I want her to be wolf. What do you want Hanna to be? I know not more than I am wolf." Nala turned her back on him and sniffed an eastern breeze.

"Hanna is on a journey, as am I." Nano stood up and faced Nala. "I need to experience the human essence through her, and I give her human contact to assist with her journey. Nala, are you sending Margaret into battle so you can be your warrior self? Will you have her sustain wounds on your behalf? Or will you free her from your shackles? Will you leave that lifetime in the past where it belongs? We need to be clear now, wolf, before we show them more, before it's too late for them to return and for us to retreat. Remember always, we are not welcome by humans. Margaret and Hanna welcome us from a place of innocence; it is their truth. Are you going to give her your lessons, or are you going to let her live her own?"

Nala growled and pawed about. She rolled on her back and shook her head; her tail curled up tight against her butt.

"*Howwwwllll*." She stood and barked at her own essence. She had chosen to become a female on earth, yet her male was still dominant in spirit. Was she both? Would s/he surrender to *Margaret*? A *human*? Would she surrender to the physicalness, the ignorance, and the innocence? Would she be able to receive as a woman? Would Nala let Margaret step and stumble, or would she pick her up midway to safety? Would she let Margaret ask the questions first, or would she answer them before Margaret knew what to ask? Would she let Margaret be innocent? She wondered whether she was indeed a female; there was a part of her that was neither female, nor was it male. There was an unresolved part of her spirit that felt neglected. This part that was ignored had turned sour from within. Nala wondered how she could care for Margaret when she wasn't sure how to care for herself. She would nurture with play and toys, not lessons. Her neglected self, a slithering serpent, would pull her out of sync; especially when she felt balanced from within, this alter self would wreak havoc and invoke her stubbornness and disdain.

Nala knew that she would have to address the darker side of herself. Disastrous events would occur if she didn't. And still, her shadow persisted by expressing disdain and disgust at the light and love Nala required to live in the physical. She didn't care if she were wolfess, goddess of wolf feminine; she didn't care who she was and what her agreements were.

Margaret watched Hanna run around in circles as she lay in the grass. She heard her calling, jumped up, and grabbed her jump rope from her book bag.

"Hanna, let's jump rope, over there on the tar."

Hanna joined her. They jumped in unison and were soon swept in by the momentum of their motion.

Margaret suddenly began to cry, and Hanna hopped out and stared at Margaret. "What's wrong, Margaret? Why are you crying?"

"I don't know," she wailed. "I don't know. I'm so sad all of a sudden. I don't know," she sobbed.

Hanna hugged her and laid her hand on her shoulder. "Aw, Margaret, I'm so sorry. I was so excited about us being twins, and when we jumped, I started to hear the music, but then you started crying. Why are you crying?"

"I told you, I don't know! My stomach kinda hurts. I just want to howl again, and yet again." Margaret was looking up to the sky, and a high-pitched sound came out of her.

The sound was so acute, Hanna held her hands to her ears. "Margaret, stop it!" she cried.

"No, no, no! I won't stop; I won't stop howling *ever*! You hear?"

Hanna was taken back a bit by Margaret's words. They were both so happy only a moment ago. And now Margaret was acting all crazy.

Nano glared at Nala. "See what you've done?"

Nala turned her back on him. She thought, *I am woman wolf, I am woman wolf, I am woman wolf. What is woman? Why? I have no body. I have no sex. Why am I woman? What do I do with woman? Grrrrrr.* She dug into the ground with her paw and pulled up some soil. She put her nose to it and took a long sniff. *Grrrrrr, brrrrr, I feel the taste; I sense this smell of soil, of earth, of woman... I sniff up to the sky and sniff the wind and know that it is male... It is male, and it explodes in the atmosphere. It rains down, the male. It is absorbed; it is received by earth. I feel now, I am the receiver, old wolf of Margaret! I see it now... I am a big hole of welcome to those of male.*

Nano lay down and watched as Nala transformed herself again and again. He knew not to interfere, to let her do her dance with her male and female selves.

She was lonely. She stood among the trees in a forest of white birch, the white-speckled narrow trunks standing one by one so close. Their branches grew perpendicular to the trunk, making space for so many. Nala was jealous of their abundance and the company they kept. *The trees are never alone*, she thought, but so lonely she was… she longed to fill her emptiness.

Her *in-between spirit* had reemerged. Nala knew that she was part of her displaced self but felt detached; she no longer clung to it, as if it were a gateway to the physical. Now that she had the physical connection, the glue seemed like a stickiness in her gut. She wanted no part of it. It caused her deep confusion within; it came from another lifetime on earth, and she knew it would not serve Margaret in this lifetime. Yet still, it was part of her.

Nala approached Nano with pride in her eyes. She stood tall, and Nano saw his wolf self in her eyes. "Yes, Nala, it is you; it is part of you. Leave it behind."

"I cannot." Nala stared at him stubbornly.

Nano knew who was talking and closed his eyes in prayer. Gently he pawed at the earth. The ground before him became a harp, and he touched the strings with his paw and strummed a chord in the key of G. It vibrated and created a heavenly feeling for the two wolves. Each time he touched the ground, the sound would resonate. Margaret heard the chord too. It was calling to her. She felt the sound in her belly; it was filling her.

Nourished now with the heavenly sound and able to hold her head high, Nala growled softly. She harmonized her growl with the chord, and a deep tone in the key of C came out. These two chords created an element in the heavens. An eight-pointed star formed in the sky above them, and the sound bounced from star point to star point.

It was here, beneath the canopy of sound and song, that Nala decided to face the sea urchin that had emerged from within her. It was an asp, and it came up from beneath. She could feel its force penetrate her, and she surrendered, trusting innocently that she could commune with this part of herself. It was rambunctious and unruly, it craved havoc and attention, and it was sorely jealous of Margaret and only wanted her death. Nala knew that she must rid herself of this entity again. She knew only that it would reemerge someday. She knew that Nano could take it away and prepared to release it to his care.

Nano had history with this entity of the opposite, the urchin with the upside-down scales, whose head grew from its tail and its tail held its brain. Nala released the chord of G again, and the heavens responded in

C. From within the merkaba of sound, the origin being the eight-pointed star, Nano called in his powers and seduced the sea urchin into his den, which sat in the center of the star. The urchin inched toward him, and he sat at ease, head held high and sniffing the cold air. Nano could feel the change of tone as the urchin drew close; it deepened and became raspy. He sang his heart out and dampened the sound of the urchin. The asp stood tall above Nano. He drooled hot oil, and his head bopped up and down, causing it to splatter and sizzle all that it touched.

Nano could smell his fur-burnt singes but held no concern. He knew that the only way to deal with this entity was to ignore it. Put yourself in its path and ignore it. It was an old battle tradition from many lifetimes ago. He would use it this time, and hopefully it wouldn't reemerge in this lifetime. He knew the key. Ignore. This enraged the serpent, and it ranted, cursing and damning every element of good and light. It created lightning and ignited it with the balls of fuel it regurgitated. It held all jealousy, and it held lies and deceptions, whose points were razor-sharp, wounding all that it touched. Nano turned his back on it and knew that it would return to the sea. He only hoped it would not come back in this lifetime.

The harmony resonated, vibrating to every direction, Margaret tried to calm herself.

Hanna sat next to her, caressing her friend's shoulder and bringing her face close to her. Hanna whispered,

> Oh sister sword, you sing your chord
> And cut through the fog of me.
> Your void—I fill
> Your heart—I will
> Be your place, to rest with me.
>
> I keep your company.
> I fill your heart.
> I know your need in me.
> I will not let us part.

Margaret stirred and smiled as Hanna whispered her words. She jumped up, grabbing Hanna's hand, and they both rose to their feet. Margaret began to sing the words too; she sang the words with Hanna. Hanna rejoiced inside. *She's singing the words! She's singing the words!*

"Come on, Margaret, let's go deliver those party invitations. Let's go and meet all of your friends! I'm so happy, I'm so happy. Let's go!" Hanna cried.

The girls left the playground and walked across the small wood bordering the park to the road where the neighborhood began.

"There are three houses on this street to find: numbers three and eight and eleven," Margaret said, looking at the envelopes. "This is a nice street."

Margaret continued to talk nonstop about the kids who lived there.

Hanna was paying attention to a corner they had passed. It was all boarded up. The whitewashed fence was tall and wrapped right around the corner; the boards had gone gray with age. As they passed it, she ran her hand over the boards. *Tick tick tick tick*, she heard the rhythm as her fingers jumped from board to board. Then she grabbed a stick and ran it across the fence as they walked, *click click click, tick tick tick*, the rhythm beating with her heart.

"Margaret, you hear that?"

"Yes, Hanna, it makes me want to jump rope with you, visit our wolves with our imagination."

"I wonder what's behind this fence."

"Dunno, it's always been like that," Margaret responded.

They arrived at number three. Margaret and Hanna approached the doorstep, and Margaret said, "This is Tom's house. He's in my grade, and he's really nice. He lets me have the ball when we are playing, and he always tells me he likes my projects in art class."

Tom's mother opened the front door, and Margaret gave her Tom's invitation. "Can he come? Can he come?" Margaret asked. "It's on Tuesday, after school."

Tom's mother smiled at the two girls and thanked them both for personally delivering the invitation. "Children, how nice of you to come to our house to deliver your birthday invitation. Thank you!"

Hanna interjected, "It's both our birthdays! We're twins! But not really; we have different parents! Oh, that's so funny." Hanna laughed and did a little dance on the small front porch of Tom's house.

"But this is Margaret's birthday party, not mine; I'm going horseback riding with my dad on Saturday for my birthday. I hope maybe Margaret can come with us," Hanna said, smiling at Margaret hopefully.

"I'll have to ask my mother, Hanna. Maybe she'll let me."

Tom's mother stepped inside the house and told Margaret that she would call her mother to let her know if they would attend the party. Then she said her good-byes.

They continued down the road to number eight as Margaret told Hanna about the next house. "This is where my mother used to take me when she went to work. She was my babysitter when I was little. I love Karolyn; she's so nice, and she just came home again because she was away at college. I hope she can come!"

Number eight was a very large house. It had a big front yard, and the girls walked up a long driveway to the front door.

Their spirits witnessed nearby, still among the white birches. Nala said, "This woman, Karolyn, she can help the girl. She can show her what it is to be a young woman—so open, so innocent, so ignorant. She can show her the difference and why she must learn this as woman knowledge."

Nano growled his approval. He nudged her side and nosed her in the ribs. "Good, good, this is good. You are catching it; you are ignorant too. I've been round this circle once before; you not. I say, I see you need help too, young Nala."

Margaret felt warm inside and happy as they rang Karolyn's doorbell. She hoped to see her. Karolyn opened the door, and Margaret rushed into her arms, jumping for joy. "Karolyn, meet my new friend, Hanna; she's my twin! Karolyn, here's my birthday party invitation. We're going to be ten. Ya know I entered fifth grade this year?"

"Wow, how time flies, Margaret. You are all grown up!" Karolyn said, looking her over and seeing how tall she'd gotten. "You may be taller than I!" she said and took the invitation. "When is it?" she asked.

"Next Tuesday, after school. Can you make it?" Margaret asked.

"I will try my best to be there, Margaret. What do you want for your birthday?"

Margaret thought for a moment; she could think of a million things! She looked up at Karolyn in adoration, slightly smug though. "Um, I know… can you make Mom let me go horseback riding with Hanna and her dad on Saturday?" She knew that Mom loved Karolyn.

Karolyn smiled. "Horseback riding? Sounds like fun. Why wouldn't she let you? Don't worry, Margaret; of course she will."

Hanna jumped up and down. "Really? Oh, I can't wait!"

Only number eleven remained. The house was slightly farther down the road, across the street. There was a cemetery in between; it took up nearly a block. The girls walked beside the black steel fence, and Hanna picked up another stick and glided it over the bars of the fence. This time it sent out more of a melody than a rhythm, and the girls began to sing their song together in unison, their chords piercing the wind that had picked up, which blew against them as they explored the gravestones.

"My mom says there's no one really here, just a load of gravestones. She said, 'When you're dead, you're dead.' There's nothing left here. But it's funny," Margaret said as she stopped and looked at a very large gravestone. She could read the big lettering all the way from the sidewalk. *Here Lie Lester and Hilda Karoo.*

"You see, each stone has a body in it. So there is something there… I'm not sure what my mom means, nothing there." Margaret stood still.

Hanna had never thought about death before, and she'd never really noticed the cemetery before. She thought to herself*, I don't even know if I've ever been on this street, with the corner with a fence around it.*

Margaret heard her thoughts and responded, "Hanna, we aren't anywhere near your house. I will probably have to show you how to get back. You probably have never been here, so why would you think about a cemetery? My mom says this is where the rich people go. The poor people get cremated; that way they don't have to pay for a grave site."

"What's *cremated*?" Hanna asked.

"I dunno. They put you in an urn, though. My mom always talks about this urn she has, for poor people 'cause they don't have money."

This was new territory for Hanna, and all she saw was a lot of new things and none of them came together.

"Oh, never mind," she said to Margaret. "Just never mind," she repeated, sounding irritated. "I think I'm gonna go home. I think I wanna skip number eleven. Can we do it tomorrow?"

"What's wrong, Hanna? Why are you mad all of a sudden?"

"I don't like death," she said. "I didn't even really know what it was. Then I see this cemetery, and you tell me all the dead people are here. I don't know. I just don't know! I need answers. And you give me answers, and they are scary, Margaret. They make me feel, what is it? They make me feel stupid. Like I don't know anything about all of these new things…"

Hanna walked off by herself in the opposite direction. Margaret followed her. They backtracked down the road, passing numbers eight and three again, and they chatted lightly about Tom and Karolyn. Hanna looked up ahead, expecting to see the boarded-up corner with whitewashed gray boards. She heard the thump of her stick on the wooden planks like before. But no. The fence was gone.

Hanna nudged Margaret with her elbow and pointed forward toward the street corner.

"Maaa, Maaagaret… um, Mar?" She stopped abruptly, then grabbed Margaret's wrist and took her forward a step.

"Margaret, *look*!"

Margaret looked in the direction Hanna was pointing. She cocked her head as she stared. She, too, stopped short, lessening the pull Hanna had on the other wrist. She grabbed Hanna and held her. "Hanna, look! How the…?"

Before them, instead of graying old whitewashed wooden boards totally concealing the street corner, there stood a small stone house. The walls, made of gray round stones, each one the size of a large ball, stood one story high, up to a white slate roof, which pointed up, with a smoking red brick chimney centered on top. The house had four windows, a green grassy yard, and a garden in full bloom. The girls stood still, their mouths open, wide-eyed and clutching at each other. They looked ahead; then they looked at each other, shocked to silence, but sudden squeals came from their lips as their stares met.

As they stood frozen in their place, a woman emerged from the front door, which was painted red, with bells hanging from its center. The bells clanged as the door opened and shut. The sound broke the freezing silence of surprise and dropped the girls back into the present. Taking very slow, very soft steps, they approached the sidewalk that led up to the woman and her doorway. She was an older woman, her hair cropped short, white, and spiky; it glistened in the sunlight. Her dress was long, and she wore many beads, which hung over her huge bustline. Her shawl looked like it was part of her dress; they noticed the beautiful beading sewn on it, and then they saw the flow of the dress, whose silky material was translucent. Light sparkled off the beads on the shawl.

The girls were hypnotized by her essence and the light show reflecting from her dress. Silently standing in total innocent curiosity, they drew in air and smelled her. They listened for any sound that would come from her and only heard her breath. *When will she talk?* they wondered. They dared not say a word and waited anxiously for her to say something.

Hanna finally broke the silence.

"Who are you? We just walked by here less than an hour ago, and this place was all boarded-up! Where did you come from?"

The woman stood solidly on her pavement. She looked at the ground; she looked to the sun, which was leaning toward the west in the late afternoon. Then she turned to the north and nodded her head. She continued to turn and nod, and then stood facing Hanna and Margaret. She was smiling brightly. Her eyes shone like bright full moons, and she had wrinkles—lots of them. Hanna looked down and saw that the woman was holding something in each one of her hands.

"Come, young ones, feel good to come and sit with me in my garden," she said to their surprise. The girls obediently followed her suggestion and sat down in her garden on white wicker chairs with cushions on them.

Once the three had sat comfortably, the woman, who was as old as their moms if not older, handed each of them a round, gray stone, each one bearing a circle marking around its middle. They looked like cracked goose eggs but were made of stone. The moment each held it in her hand, they felt inclined to close their eyes. Hanna flew away on her Nano's back to the stars; Margaret stood face-to-face with Nala, seeing the struggle about to occur.

"Not now, girls. Now is not the time to dream. Put down your stones on the table while we talk," the woman said, and the girls followed her command.

"Who are you?" Hanna asked for the fourth time. "Why weren't you here when we passed by here earlier?"

"Oh, but I was, darling young girl. I've been here for a very long time."

"Why did you have a fence around your house?" Margaret spoke up finally. "We came by here, and there was a fence, only an hour ago! How did you get it down so fast?"

"Hmmm." The woman picked up one of the stones and looked deeply into it, and then she looked up and stared at the girls intensely. "Sometimes what you think you see isn't necessarily what is really there. Today you walked by this corner, and you were focusing on where to go to deliver your invitations. You were not open, and you were clearly thinking about what was before you and not what was in front of you."

"Sooooo?" Hanna argued. "We still saw the fence."

"Maybe it wasn't a fence; maybe it was a barrier for you. Maybe you needed to beat on it with your stick to make it real; otherwise, you may have seen my house."

"Wait a minute," Margaret said. "You saw us pass by before?"

"Oh yes, and I heard you talking about your birthday."

Both of them looked at each other and wanted to bolt with fright. They nodded at each other, and on a mental count of three, they jumped up and ran as fast as they could away from the stone house, the green grass, and the woman who sat in her yard. They could hear her laughing for as far as they could run. Out of breath, they slowed down and came to a stop, right outside the playground where they met.

Hanna needed to go home as it was getting late, but Margaret wanted to stop and talk some more.

"Hanna, what's going to happen to us? We keep seeing and hearing all this stuff; I know it's not normal. This doesn't happen to other kids, or we would have heard about it in school or at the park, don't you think?"

"Margaret, I'm tired, and I'm still frightened. I know we will see her again. I know we have no control of this, just like we are twins and just found out today. I feel like we are on the edge of knowing something, but we don't know what. I wish we had someone to talk to about this!"

Margaret turned to Hanna. "I'm going to tell my mother. I think she'll understand. She read me so many fairy tales when I was little about all kinds of things that disappeared and reappeared… like the book called *Where the Wild Things Grow*. About animals that talk to each other, and plants and trees that come to life! Maybe she will believe me. Maybe I can tell her I'm writing a story, and then write a short story about what we are seeing and show it to her. But I want to tell her tonight! I won't have time to write it down."

"It's okay, Margaret." Hanna sat down on the grass and played with a blade. She held it up to the sky and said, "You see this? The green of this blade of grass, the blue of the sky, you see how that's so beautiful? Well, these things we see are the same thing."

"Hanna, what are you talking about? You've gone crazy with all this. I'm talking about my mother, and what's that got to do with grass and the sky?"

"Simple, Margaret. Do you tell your mom every time you see something surprising or beautiful? Do you sit down with her and ask her about it all? Or don't you like just to wonder and dream about it, and not share it, 'cause they'll just ruin it?"

"Ah, Hanna, I get it. Hmmm, okay, so we need to talk about this a lot then, 'cause I just can't keep it to myself."

"Why *don't* you write about it? That was your idea, and I think it's a good one!"

"I'll have to get a notebook to write in, and a new pen! We don't have a typewriter at home. Do you?"

"Yeah, upstairs in the study, there's a typewriter. My dad sits in there and types sometimes at night. I hear it 'cause it's next to my bedroom," Hanna said, and wondered if Margaret could come to her house to write. "I can ask my mom if you can come over."

"Or I can just write it in a notebook. That seems good for me, and then I can lie on my bed and in the yard under the maple tree and write." Margaret felt better and more content. The fear had dissipated, and the two girls felt peaceful again.

"I guess we should go home. It's pretty late. The sun is going down, and we better hurry." Hanna stood up and pulled Margaret to her feet. "So, it's a deal? You aren't going to say anything about anything to your mom, right?" Hanna asked.

"Yeah, okay," Margaret responded reluctantly, staring down at the ground.

"Margaret? Really!" Hanna stamped her foot and frowned. "It's okay," she said. "I'm going home."

"Good night. Tomorrow we have more invitations to deliver. I hope we don't discover any new houses again!"

Hanna walked down the lane to her house nearby. Her thoughts took her to the yard and how she was going to not count. She would hold it in, try and breathe, but hold it in—the numbers, the counting. It made her anxious just thinking about it, yet she her body yearned for that angst feeling in her stomach, and the stiffness in her throat. *Just walk*, she thought; *think about happy things.* As she approached the stairs, she thought that Dad would be in a good mood. He would laugh and give her a big hug when she got in. Mom would just smile and pat her head as she passed. It would all be okay—no bad news to hear, and no surprises from them today, she hoped.

There. She was nearing her front yard and her turn right up the hill to the house onto the pavement of slate and moss; she felt the urge to say one, to count.

"No, just say a color!" she heard something say.

Hanna turned to the voice. A color? Red! And another color… say, yellow! Hanna thought loudly in her brain to wash out the angst. Blue, she called almost out loud. And she smiled inside as the colors replaced the numbers, and somehow they weren't so bad. She wondered who that voice was as she approached the porch steps and felt the urge to count again. Gray, she thought out loud.

"Hanna, did you say gray?" her mother asked.

"Yeah, Mom, I was thinking about these steps. When are we going to paint them? You can see the gray wood, and since when is wood gray?"

Hanna's mom smiled and patted her on the head as she'd hoped. Inside, she subsided, knowing there were no announcements or meetings tonight. A pat on the head for Hanna meant everything is okay. Like with Mom. Sometimes Mom was scary, but tonight she was in a good mood, and that relaxed Hanna. Mom was cooking by the smell of the roast chicken and the fact that Dad was not yet home. This gave her time to go to her room and lie down for a while, one of her favorite things to do at home.

Hanna loved her bedroom. Tonight she lay there on the bed staring up at the ceiling, which had a wooden molded centerpiece that held the lightbulb. The centerpiece was painted blue, and it reminded her of the colors she had just thought of in the front yard. *Why did the colors soothe me so when the numbers caused me to feel so uptight and frightened?* Hanna wondered. Then she remembered that she wanted to color. It had been a few years since she had colored in a coloring book, but it felt good to choose each color and to stay within the lines. She chose a picture of a stone house and began to color in the round stones in hues of gray, pink, and purple. The colors blended nicely; they made her feel good in her belly.

Soon enough, Hanna's mother called her down for dinner; Dad had come home and was very quiet. He hadn't even gone up to her room to say hi. This was a sign to her that she should eat her food real quick and get out of the kitchen. Otherwise, Dad would jump on anything she said, even if it were the best thing in the world. She knew all too well what happened when she opened her mouth. She thought, *Hanna, what are you doing?* but she kept talking.

"Dad, something strange happened to me today. Dad, can I tell you about it?"

Jay glared at her from across the table; Mom put down her fork and looked up from her food.

"I was walking with Margaret today, Dad. You remember that you said I could go horseback riding for my birthday? Well, Dad, Margaret's my twin!" She blurted it out and then waited. The silence that followed felt like a year to Hanna as she held her breath.

Jay continued to glare at her and said, "A twin, eh? I don't remember having a twin." He looked at Mom and asked, "Carol, do you remember having twins when Hanna was born?"

Mom nodded silently.

Hanna was still holding her breath, and there was food in her mouth. She held her napkin to her mouth and spat out the food. She put her arm in front of her plate and rested her forehead on it; she didn't want to hear him.

"What do you think, Carol? Is Hanna being delusional again, acting all crazy? A twin. How did you come up with that stupid idea?"

Hanna lifted her head and felt rage in her stomach. It was rising quickly up her chest into her throat, and she felt the tears welling in her eyes.

"Oh, Dad, you're so mean to me. What would you do if I told you I saw a house appear out of nowhere today? What would you do if I told you I see wolves flying in the air and they talk to me?" She slid off her chair and stood yelling at him.

Then her body told her to get out of the room, and she darted out of the kitchen backdoor into the yard. She ran to the grass and threw herself to the softness, burying her head in the fragrant ground. She waited silently, trying to make herself disappear in the overgrown grass.

Jay came tearing out of the house murmuring to himself, "I'm going to get to the bottom of this! Hanna, get yourself over here. What kind of talk is this? You know I've had a hard day in the office. Why are you causing all this drama? Who is this twin anyway? What kind of stupid things are you seeing? Do you want us to go see the doctor? Find out what's wrong with you? Why aren't you normal, like Michal?"

"Michal's boring," Hanna said quietly and sat up, still looking down, afraid to meet his stabbing eyes. When she looked at him, she felt like he was hitting her. She waited for the next verbal blow to come, but it didn't. Dad had gone back indoors, and she was left to herself.

Oh good, she thought, *he's too tired. Phew, that was a close one. Why did I say all that stuff?* she wondered.

She lay back down and stared at the sky, noticing that there were two big black crows perched on the tree. They were looking down at her, and the moment she looked up, they began to caw, long drawn-out ones, like they were talking to her, but she didn't know why. They cocked their heads back and forth and knocked their beaks in her direction. Abruptly, Hanna stood to her feet and yelled out at them, "What?" What do you want from me?"

The crows shut up and flew off.

That night Hanna dreamed of the crows again. They knew her wolves and they knew the old lady they had met and they knew Margaret. Her dream took her to a place where they were all together, living in a green forest that smelled of moss and earth and flowers. She followed the scent and found a pond, with fresh lotus flowers blossoming on the surface. She sat down on the muddy bank on a rock so as not to get her bottom wet. The water glistened as it flowed by, and Hanna found herself staring at the reflection and the shadow of the water in its movement. The momentum drew her closer to the surface, and she found her consciousness slipping into the water and flowing and tumbling and rolling down the creek, which had appeared out of nowhere. Just like the stone house.

Margaret's dreams took her to the same pond; they were both as surprised as the other when they found themselves sitting on its bank. They were now both flowing together down the creek that had appeared out of nowhere; they found themselves not in the water but gliding along on a raft. The crows were perched on each of their shoulders, and the wolves were lounging all stretched out in the middle of the raft, away from the water. The old woman was sitting on her own yard chair, which Margaret remembered from the day before. She had cookies and called them both round to sit by her. The old woman began to sing. The girls recognized the melody from the song the wolves were teaching them. She had new words.

And when the skies become so dark
We strain our eyes to see,
Release your heart and let it start
To see like eyes—a hawk eyed view
Of how to turn the tides anew.

Bring them forward, flip them back,
Your strength your biggest flaw,
Your flaw your biggest strength.
Spirals and reflects,
The mirrors of our breath.

The girls sang the song, backed up by howls and caws, while the old woman banged a heartbeat rhythm with a wooden spoon on the arm of her chair.

Chapter 3

"They are progressing." Nano nudged Nala and growled softly.

"Aye, wolf, they are. They found the woman you sent them," she responded.

"And Margaret could see her, too. I am grateful, wolf, you gave her, you let her. This is good."

Nano gazed at Nala and nodded his head. She growled again, this time with more emotion. How she yearned for Margaret to learn her lessons for her, but she knew she needed herself to learn them first. Margaret had her own lessons, and the old woman would help her. Nala surrendered to the twist in her heart and tried to let it out with a wrenching howl into the heavens. She knew she would soon feel all of that pain bouncing back to her threefold and got ready to dodge it. Pulling all of her energies around her, she created a circle of light and comfort.

She sat and saw her demons eyeing their target—her. She squirmed and fell and tossed on the ground among the dry leaves. Their crackling sent her imagination to the horrid sounds she heard among the demons. Her tall goddess stood before her, and she called to her from a million miles away. "I'm here, sweet goddess, please come and get me. Please bring me back from here." And her goddess stood firm and watched. The flashes of thunder and lightning surrounded Nala. She let her heart project the biggest love she could muster. She let her visions bring her rainbows and glistening crystals, and still the reverberations of her howl continued to find their source. As they returned like daggers, she held up her shield of light and let them bounce off and fall into the atmosphere and down to the mothering earth plane, where they found cleansing and refreshment. Their hunger for earth and soil and nurturing was satisfied, and they renewed themselves again among the beings of light.

Nala watched and listened; she recognized herself in the light, and it was from here she could teach her little human on earth. It was from here she could bring her a fruitful life, full of newness and lessons and gateways to the great spirit of all.

Nano sat and witnessed his mate's journey. He was elated with her progress, as well as the progress of the two girls. The girls were about to embark on their first real journey, which would show them how to blend the two worlds gracefully. They had just celebrated their joint twin birthday party and were saying good-bye to the final guests. Hanna stayed to help Margaret and her mother clean up; she'd told her parents she would walk home.

The party was a great success. They both received lots of gifts that they were dying to go and check out, but instead, they cleared out all of the paper plates and cups and leftover food and cake from the communal yard where the party was held, taking it upstairs to Margaret's apartment. Margaret's mother was washing dishes in the kitchen and thanked the children for their help. "It's your birthday, young ladies, each of you ten years old. Go out and have fun! Margaret, please be sure to be home before dark."

The girls grinned, staring into each other's beaming eyes.

"Yes!" they said in unison and skipped out of the kitchen. "Let's gather up our presents and go to the swings to look them over! Let's take the jump rope too!" Margaret's voice was full of joy as she went to find a bag. They gathered up their gifts into one bag and took off down the road toward the creek.

When they reached the creek, there was a fork in the path. One way led to the playground, and the other led to the street where the two had met the old woman and her disappearing and reappearing house. Hanna and Margaret looked at each other with mischief, knowing full well they weren't going to the playground, and veered off to the old woman's house.

"Do you think the house will be there, Margaret?" Hanna asked. "I mean, just because we saw it once doesn't mean we'll see it again. What was it she said? We need to be open to it? Like we accept the dreams we have? What do you think?"

"It's not a matter of what you think, dear child; it's a matter of where you feel it and what you can learn from that!" The voice came from all around them, and the girls twirled the four directions to see where it was coming from. They hadn't quite reached the neighborhood with the house on the corner, and yet they felt and could hear this woman.

"She sounds so scary!" Margaret whispered to Hanna.

"Why can we hear her?" Hanna responded, standing still facing Margaret. "Margaret, I have an idea. Let's jump rope! Let's see what we see; let's see if we hear the song! Then we will know if this is right. What do you think?"

"I think we shouldn't have brought all of our presents with us. They may get heavy if we have to run real fast all of a sudden."

"You want to leave them here?"

"Look, we can hide them over there near the creek under that tree trunk. There's a place I know," Margaret said, walking down off the path toward the creek.

"What if someone finds them and takes them, Margaret?" Hanna hesitated and stood in her tracks. "I don't know about this."

And then they both heard the old woman's voice again. "You and your gifts will be safe, young'uns. Come along now; time is short."

Margaret and Hanna looked at each other.

"Let's take the bag with us, Mar. Here, I'll carry it!" Hanna said and picked up the bag.

"Hanna, everything inside of me is telling me to run! But there's this thing in my stomach. It's like butterflies; it's so exciting! I am so curious. Come on; let's run there!" Margaret declared.

The two ran back onto the path, forked toward the old woman's voice and her reappearing house, and came upon the corner more quickly than they remembered.

"There it is!" Margaret pointed. There were no signs of any boarding or fence; the grass was green around the house, and the woman's flower beds were blooming. The sun glistened off the walls of the stone house.

Hanna felt an urge to count the stones. When she felt the urge to count again, she thought, *so that's what it is. I count when I approach the unknown.* Amazed at such a thought, she looked forward and ran toward the house ignoring her urges and freeing herself from their clutches.

"Hello, young ladies," the old woman said as they approached her front yard. "Have you come to visit me this time? What have you brought with you, dear girls?" The woman smiled warmly at them and motioned her hand to the big bag Hanna was carrying. "I'm sorry; I haven't introduced myself—how rude of me."

She rose from her comfy deck chair, not too high, not too low. She was a well-set woman with round hips and a tiny waist, her legs covered by a long pink and purple flowery skirt. On top she wore a purple poncho. She wore cowboy boots—dark purple ones. Well-polished. Her hair was silver gray with purple highlights; she wore it loose, and it flowed down her back, the purple shining and blending with the silver. The reflective rays blinded Hanna and Margaret, and they shaded their eyes to see better where they were walking directly into the bright sunrays.

"My name is Trudy Goodenough, and what are your names? So very nice to meet you." She reached out her hand, shook theirs, and then cradled each of their foreheads in her hands and kissed them.

"Hi!" Margaret drew back from her hands and pointed. "This is my friend, Hanna, and my name is Margaret. We're not supposed to talk to strangers, but you seem okay."

Hanna added, "Yeah, we're not supposed to speak to you." She looked down at the old woman's dark purple cowboy boots and noted the pointy sharp toes. They had silver tips on them.

The girls put their heads together for a moment and whispered. "Let's just stay for a minute. We won't go in the house; we'll just stay here outside. That should be okay."

They turned to Trudy, who had sat down and was playing with a small crystal in her hand.

"So, Mrs. Goodenough, we have decided that it's okay if we sit with you outside for a little while," Hanna stated. "It's our birthday today. We're twins."

"Well, happy birthday! We must have cake! I will bring some out." She got up with a spring and bounced up to her house.

"She seems nice, Margaret, I think she's okay. But why can we hear her like we hear our wolves? Like when we can't see her. How did she make her voice so loud in our heads?"

"Maybe we should ask her," Margaret said.

When the woman returned carrying a tray with two plates of cake, forks, and two glasses of milk, Hanna asked, "Aren't you having some?"

"Oh, I had mine just a while ago; must watch my figure, you know."

"Mrs. Goodenough, we have a question." Margaret stood up from her chair. "When we were coming down the lane today, we could hear your voice in the woods by the creek—the one with the white birch. Were you there with us? How could we hear you and not see you? And we could hear you, but I don't think anyone else could hear you, just us. How is that, Mrs. Goodenough? Why do you speak to us inside? It's like when we jump rope almost."

"Jump rope?" Trudy asked.

"Yes, ma'am! When we jump rope, we can see things and hear things, things that aren't here on earth. So when we heard you in the woods before we came here, it was the same kind of sound, like, not from here. We don't know where from, Mrs. Goodenough. We don't know." Margaret looked down and felt sorry and confused; not knowing was very hard for her.

"Well, girls, perhaps I can help you along the way. These things you see? Do you see them, or do you feel them?"

"Both," they said in unison, and giggling.

Hanna continued, "It's like it's all over, inside and outside, but our imagination is all it is, but it feels real and we know it's real because we both see and hear the same thing!"

"So, Mrs. Goodenough, do you know what it is?" Margaret asked.

"What does the jump rope do? Is it like a magic wand?" Hanna pursued.

Both girls were throwing questions at the woman, who sat quietly with her hands folded, smiling contently at them. Her gaze was powerful, and both girls began to feel it. Eventually their questioning subsided, and they simply sat. They were both staring into the woman's eyes; their gaze pulled them into her as she allowed her vision to be seen.

A panoramic view appeared before the girls; it was a projection coming from Trudy's eyes. They could not believe what they saw, and yet they continued to stare. A green meadow appeared in front of them. It was full of animals comingling and frolicking in the warm sunlight. The two girls stood at the edge, near the wood. They watched the animals all playing together. There were tigers chasing butterflies, and instead of eating them, they were allowing the butterflies to settle on their noses, sillily sitting cross-eyed while a big black bear out there far across the meadow was pawing gently at a lamb, trying to get her to chase him. An eagle was sitting on a raccoon's back, and they nosed each other affectionately. The girls could hear a chorus of bird calls, all merging into an uplifting harmony, which added color to the landscape. Then Trudy began to speak, and the girls listened intently.

"I come from far away and up close. I am, I will be, and I was. We live in a world of many dimensions, and I travel among them. I was born on the east coast of the Russian Baltic Sea, in a small village of natives of this northern land. We fished for our food in the freezing sea and gathered any edible fruit that the rough terrain could offer. Even today, I feel the gratitude within me for the fruits of our mother earth.

"I traveled far when I was young; my father found work on the American fishing ships, and he brought us here to America. My mother reminded me throughout my life that I would be the one to carry the family story to the next people—the story of our native people, not Russian folk; we came from an inuit people who live a sacred existence with mother earth and all of the powers that be. My mother would tell me the lesson in everyday life and make me look for my own lessons with my prayers each night.

"When I grew to be a young woman, we were in America and there were no suitors for me, so I created a life of learning and gathering of my tribal roots. I found a place here in America where I can come and go as I wish within the dimensions that coexist here. I have learned to live in my attention and my dream at the same time. I took education with all of the western religions. I was a nun and a worker for the monks. I did missionary services for the Christian leagues in the Middle East and the villages of Palestine before they called it Israel. That's when I began to see the hatred and evil between the religions and knew that mine was not religion, but a way of life, a path of heart and light. I knew that it was so alien to those who believed in religion that I could not share it with them. They would judge me and think me conceited and bloated with ego; they would not see my spirit self.

"And so, I have lived a fairly lonely life of wisdom, and I am ready to share with you two young girls. You two, who have so very deliberately been chosen to hear these teachings. I hope they will assist you on your path."

The girls had finished their cake and were fidgeting in their seats. They wanted to sit and listen to the old woman, but they were shifting and giggling.

The old woman felt their young impatience and knew just what to do. "Here, girls, I have a game for you! Why don't you both sit down on the grass here and empty out your bag? Let's see what you have in there. Then I want you to spend some time with each present. Close your eyes and feel your thankfulness, your gratitude; give a few moments to the person who gave you this gift. Why would they give you this gift? What was their intent? Was there something to learn from it? Spend some time with each item, young ladies."

Hanna was slightly dazed from the story and from the image of the meadow that they had seen from the old woman's eyes. She sat in her chair as Margaret happily jumped up and spilled out the contents of their birthday gift bag onto the grass. Most of the presents had not yet been opened, and Hanna's curiosity caught her as she saw the wrapped gifts pile out of the bag. She loved the wrapping and carefully removed it from a box tagged with her name. After she had neatly folded the last bit of wrapping, she watched Margaret tear hers open, flip the box, and let the gift fall out. It was a small bag with bath soap in it.

Hanna diverted her attention back to her gift; it was from her dad. He had already given her the main gift at home—the horseback riding trip—but this was another one! Hanna's heart skipped a beat at the thought; she never received gifts from Dad, and today there were two! Her heart opened as she allowed her love for him into the call of her very being. She felt her love for him from her toes to the tips of her ears, and the music then floated up through her brain and made her blush. Tears came to her eyes as she stopped a moment with her finger about to pull open the box. She loved her dad so; her love was deep and intense, and her fear of him was equally so. How could that be? Maybe the answer was in the box.

Hanna popped open the box and found a silver bracelet inside. She picked it up and saw the charms drop down: a star, a heart, a pen, and a silver label with her name on it. Hanna's jaw dropped as she saw her favorite symbols tied to the silver braided chain. She shot her wrist out to Margaret, holding the bracelet up. "Oh, Margaret, look, look what my dad gave me. Will you put it on me, please?" Her answer had come; he had given her symbols of his love in ways she could understand. He had reached her, and she reached to him with her heart. Then suddenly, she saw another charm hiding near the clasp; it was a silver wolf with turquoise eyes, an open mouth, and a nose pointed to the stars. "Look, everyone," she cried, "a howling wolf! How does Dad know about the wolves?"

Trudy looked up from the bracelet into Hanna's eyes. "Tell me about your wolves, Hanna. Margaret, do you see them too?"

"Oh yes, especially when we jump rope!" they said in unison with bright smiles.

Margaret felt relieved to be asked about the wolves; Hanna couldn't wait to tell Trudy more.

"They sing to us a song, and every time it has new words! They kind of dance with us and let us sit on their backs, and then they fly. Right now, we have only had fun with them; we don't really talk to them. Isn't that right, Margaret?"

Hanna looked to Margaret for an answer. Instead, Margaret began to sing the song, and all became quiet as her soft tingling voice sounded around them. They all closed their eyes, listening intently.

Trudy's spirit animal greeted the wolves. He was a tall tan elk, with long legs and fully grown antlers. He bowed to the wolves and again to the star; he hoofed around a bit and circled round Trudy. The girls' spirit wolves sat up and stared up at the elk towering over them. Its calm energy enveloped them, and they knew they were in the presence of an old one, an ancient spirit who had much to teach, and they paid attention.

Hanna and Margaret sat back down in their chairs. Trudy was in a deep state, her eyes closed; her hands shook slightly. They all paid close attention to the elk. He sang:

> *The four-legged stood tall and stalked*
> *Round the ones who heard his call.*
> *He knew his spot, at every dot.*
>
> *In the south he ate*
> *And fed his body of length and strength.*
> *And in the west his dream was felt.*

In the north he called in the wild and spirit of himself,
Seeing, seeing, seeing
The eastern vision of his dream, now his thought, he stalked.

"North? South? What's he talking about? Are we going somewhere?" Margaret asked.

Trudy slowly opened her eyes and eventually responded, but only after Margaret repeated the question numerous times.

"Children, you are young. You are hearing new things; just let them settle. Don't ask too many questions right now. Maybe the answers will come by themselves; maybe you will see for yourselves what this is and why the elk speaks of the four directions. Try it yourself, young'un. Sit with the sunset in the west one day; get the feeling and see how it arouses your feelings and your dreams. This is good. Now it is time for you to go; it's starting to get dark."

The girls split up their presents to take home. Most were unopened still, and they really didn't care. There would be time to open them at home. Trudy gave them an extra bag; it was strange-looking, made of purple velvet. They had a lot to think about.

A Wolf Song

Quiet and tired, Margaret and Hanna each gave Trudy a hug and started off down the path into the woods and the creek. They walked quickly and silently, each of them in her own world, her own thoughts and dreams.

As Hanna approached her front yard, the usual anxiety came up. As happy as she was as she dangled the sparkling silver charms from the bracelet that her dad had given her, she wondered if she could trust it. Would he be nice to her tonight, or would he be mean? Would he yell at her for coming home so late? Two, four, six, eight, ten, twelve, fourteen, sixteen… She resented it, though she still found herself counting, this time in twos, more powerful, two whole numbers for each. Her thought stopped. *For each what?*

Hanna was dumbfounded that all of a sudden, she didn't know what for anymore. The numbers had no value to her; there was nothing there. They had disappeared, just like the reappeared house.

Hanna picked up her head, brought her walk up to a bouncing skip, and started singing "Happy Birthday to me," as she sprung up the front path. Mom was on the porch and joined in with Hanna to the song. She stood to greet Hanna today, not with the normal pat on the head, but gave her a big hug, holding her close to her breast. Hanna rested there for a moment, feeling the warmness and the love. She felt relieved to know that all was well at home.

"Hanna," her mom said, "you missed dinner. We didn't expect you till now—you're not late—but would you like some dinner? I put a plate in the oven for you. It's your favorite, spaghetti and meatballs."

"Oh yeah, I'm so hungry, Mom, thank you!"

"Don't forget to use the oven gloves," Mom called.

Later that night, Margaret was in an inferno. Fire trucks were parked outside and pouring shots of water onto her house, and her mother was standing outside with all of the neighbors and other firemen and policemen. She stood still as the picture began to unfold. Stunned, shocked, and blown over, her body wavered back and forth; she wondered if she would fall. The smoke smelled horrible; she tried to hold her breath and couldn't. Tears welled in her eyes, and her chest felt as if it wanted to burst open.

She heard herself wailing aloud. "Maaaaamaaaa," she cried. Her mom turned to see her and ran over. Margaret ran into her arms and held tight, closing her eyes tightly against her mother's side rib, feeling the pain on her forehead from her mother's bones. "Maaaaaa!" she continued to wail.

Her wails were heard on the other side by her wolf spirit as howls in the wind, pulling her toward her physical kin as she came from deep slumber. She rolled about pawing at her snout and scrubbing her forehead, as if she felt the pressure of the mother's rib too. A wave of grief came up her throat, and she let out a howling release, which the child felt too. Margaret knew within her as she hugged her mother and hid her face against her bony frame, and spirit wolf who felt the same, she knew they were two and they were one. Margaret knew she was not alone and could now peek out at the wreckage and listen to the noise of the fire trucks as their water made dents in her house, knocking burned-out planks aside.

But then both of her, Margaret and Nala, looked down into the depths of her home, flooded, charred, and ridden with empty grief. *It's all gone*, was all she could muster in her thoughts… *It's all gone… it's gone. Empty. What else is there?* "Ohhhhhhh, Maaaaaaaaa," she cried up at her mom and said, "What now, Mom? Where will we sleep tonight? What will we do, Mom?"

Margaret collapsed on the ground, and her mother fell with her. Both were scooped up by paramedics and taken to a nearby ambulance, where an angelic-looking woman sat inside. Margaret opened her eyes into the woman's green glistening sea of compassion and was enveloped by it. She felt herself smiling softly at her and watched the thought go through her head. *Is this an angel?* The woman responded to her. "Ah, so you think I'm an angel, do you?" Her voice sounded like a thousand songbirds; Margaret could feel the sound of it vibrate inside and out. "Are you real?" Margaret heard herself ask, as if in a dream she were. The woman replied, "Of course, I'm real. Are you?"

Margaret laughed at her silliness and tried to sit up. She was on a stretcher inside the ambulance. Her mother was not with her, and as she looked around to search, the woman said, "Your mother is in the next vehicle, darling. Not to worry; she is fine. We'll have to see you get some dinner, what do you think?"

Margaret wasn't hungry and asked to see her mother.

"Well, let's give her some time, dear one. Would you like a Twinkie? I think I may have one here in my lunch bag."

"No, I don't want a Twinkie, thank you. Can I go to my friend's house? It's her birthday too today."

The woman's green eyes brightened and her face lit up. "What a wonderful idea! What is your name, young lady? My name is Isabella. I live not far from here. Maybe I can take you to your friend's house."

"I need to ask my mother, and where's my mother going to go?"

"Darling, why don't you lie down for a few more minutes, and I'll go talk to your mother."

Margaret put her head on the pillow, which scrunched and made a bunch of noise, and let herself merge with her spirit wolf. She felt good there for a few moments, warm and safe within her fur and heartbeat sound.

Nala spoke to her. "You are in the dreamtime, Margaret. You are living out your deepest fears here in the safeness of the dreamtime. There are folk across the seas who call it the dreamtime; you can too and some day you will meet the aborigines of Australia."

Hanna was just finishing up her spaghetti when she felt herself being called from above. Nano was barking and jumping about and tearing up tree trunks from either side. She couldn't ignore his calls and silently put her plate in the sink and crept up to her room to be in solitude. She settled herself in her closet in the dark, with the slightest of light seeping through the keyhole and under the door. Hanna stared into the keyhole's light and saw her wolf spirit loud and clear. He was very upset, and she honed in on him and tried to touch him with her fingertip.

Then she heard Margaret's voice. She was crying in distress. Hanna felt a pull in her belly, her throat swelling in her unknown. She squeezed her eyes shut and concentrated on Nano. She asked inside, "What's happening to Margaret? What can I do? She's calling me."

Nano spoke quietly. He rambled on a bit; he spoke about dreams and time. "Little one, you are in her space and she in yours; you are in total sync if you would only trust yourself. Margaret is dreaming, my dear. She is having a, what you call on earth, a nightmare. Her house is burning, her life is burning, and she is trying to reach you. She has a guardian angel with green eyes who is guiding her. Send her love, my love. Send her love. See her in her beauty, out of fear, with courage and spirit! See her, Hanna!" Nano had stood up and was staring into Hanna's eyes as he stated again, very clearly, "See her, Hanna."

"What if we were separated?" Hanna asked. The thought created an endless stream of ache and sorrow in her belly. She quickly dispelled such a thought and felt better.

Nano said, "Hanna, be careful what you think, especially now, you are so linked with Margaret... See her, Hanna; send her love. She needs you now in this dreamtime."

There; he'd said it. *Dreamtime*. He wasn't sure if she would recognize this word or place or where.

Margaret was tossing and yelling in her sleep and had drawn her mother's attention. She was still cleaning up from the afternoon birthday party. The vacuum had been on and she hadn't heard, but she felt her daughter's calling. When she reached the bedroom, Margaret was in an awful state, with tearstained pillow and cheek, sweaty from head to toe. Worn-out and forlorn, this child was limp and stuck in the unknown of her dream. Awake, yet still in the nightmare.

She felt her friend now, and she felt her mother's gaze. These streams of light interfered with her horror and shock; Isabella became faint in her memory and the smell of smoke evaporated before her. Hanna was jumping rope. Hanna was near the swings, those seats of choice, where her power knew when to jump and she was confident to take every step without hesitation. Ahhh, it was Hanna, and she relaxed.

Her mother watched a calm come over her daughter as she opened her eyes with a smile.

"Oh, Mom, what a dream I just had! Mom, do you have Hanna's telephone number? I have to call her now!"

"Margaret, it's late, too late to make phone calls. You can call her in the morning."

Margaret said, "No, Mom, I have to, I have to."

Her mother, convinced that Margaret would not let her be for a moment until she provided the number, reconsidered and acted on her daughter's wishes, thinking, *it's still her birthday, and Hanna's too.*

A Wolf Song

The telephone rang at Hanna's home. It was past nine o'clock, and Jay answered the phone.

"Hello?" Margaret said shyly. "May I please speak with Hanna, sir?" Margaret had never spoken with him, only heard Hanna's stories about her dad.

"Don't you think it's kinda late, young lady?" was the response.

Margaret nearly hung up, fearful of the next sentence, not wanting to hear. She repeated, "May I please speak with Hanna?"

"Listen, young lady, what's your name? I said it's too late. You do speak English? What don't you understand?"

"It's very urgent," she peeped, wondering if he would hear her beneath his bellowing.

"Urgent? What can be urgent in a ten-year–old's life?"

"My house just burned down," Margaret lied and smiled in discomfort while she squirmed in her seat.

Her mother turned and glared at her.

There was silence at the other end of the telephone line.

Hanna had heard the telephone ring but had not heard it ring off; she wondered who had called so late. She tiptoed into her parents' bedroom and carefully picked up the receiver to listen in.

"Let me speak with your mother *immediately*!" she heard.

Margaret handed the phone to her mother automatically, and her Joan proceeded to explain that Margaret had just had a nightmare while napping She made her apologies, and Hanna was too scared to pipe up, even though she urgently wanted to speak with Margaret.

"Hey, Dad, since it's our birthday still and Margaret had a bad dream, do you think we can talk for a few minutes?" Hanna couldn't believe her courage. She held her breath waiting for the blow. And right she was. There was silence on the line as she heard the heavy crunches climbing up the stairs toward the bedroom. She knew he was coming for her, and she didn't know what to do. "Margaret, I love you! I have to go; Dad's coming."

She heard Margaret's voice as she hung up, ready to bolt from under him. "Hanna? Are you okay?"

She just sat there waiting. Would it come from behind, or would he pick her up and slap her up front? She winced thinking about it

"Hannaaaaaa!" he yelled as he arrived.

"Um, sorry, Dad. I just knew it was Margaret. I just knew, sorry, didn't mean to cut into your phone call. Well, it was mine actually…"

"*Yours?*" Outraged, he shouted, "Nothing is yours. You are a child. It's all mine. If you are good, you have certain privileges, do you hear? *Nothing, and I say nothing,* is yours when you're ten."

"Sorry, Dad."

He'd clipped her under the ear as he shouted, and it stung. Her hearing became different; his voice became more distant. Her head spun, and she closed her eyes to make it stop. She also heard her mom coming up the stairs and knew that he would leave her alone the moment Mom stepped in the room. Hanna waited and made herself cry, trying to buy time so he wouldn't hook her again.

Hanna's mom strolled into the room as if nothing were happening. She looked directly across, through her husband, with icy eyes and said, "Look, Hanna, the full moon is shining out the window. Why don't you go outside and take a better look at it? I know how you love the moon!" She smiled, staring Jay in the eye while her words shot out like arrows toward his skull.

The sound of her loveful voice pulled Hanna out of her petrified state, and she darted out the door, down the stairs, and out the front door onto the porch. From the safety of her porch, she stood and felt the warm light emanating from the full moon. It felt blue to her, and she felt blue inside. Why was her dad like that? Her ear ached.

At this moment, she felt a growing ball of gratitude in her throat, nearly bringing her to tears again. But these were different tears. She knew she had her wolf and Trudy and Margaret and her mom (sometimes); this made her feel safer, and she cried her thanks. She didn't know how to express gratitude and only knew the polite words of thank you. Now she felt gratitude and what it did for her belly and her heart. It filled them like Thanksgiving dinner.

The birthday for age ten was a monumental birthday. It marked the end of their first decade. Where would they be in ten years?

Chapter 4

Trudy Goodenough had had a good day. Finally, after ten years of waiting, she had met the girls! Her relationship with the wolves had intensified in recent months, and it was at her urging that they finally brought the girls together and introduced themselves around the jump rope.

She tidied up the front garden where they had sat; she brought in the chairs and folded them against the front of the stone house, where the awning stood to keep things out of the rain. She felt their young and bright light still lingering like bubbles not yet popped, full of their innocent joy. Trudy smiled to herself and absorbed the playful light; she began to hum.

> Oh, Elk, who stands with me
> And shares your love and words,
> Your wisdom flows through
> The branches of your chords, the leaves of your voice.
> We hold the trunk of your being within us.

And the wolves joined in howling; the two were barking up at the sky of skies, and the sun set with colors of purple and violet golden rays streaming from the source. Trudy watched the light shine before her and sensed the wolves circling her ether body; she felt their true essence deep within.

"Old woman." Nano nosed her shoulder.

She shifted her position, her listening ear aimed toward what he was about to say.

"Now that our bodies have felt you, we can be grateful. It is good, oh Trudy, woman of fish and the winged ones. Your elk tells us of his song, and we see the girls too. They are coming to a rough journey. Woman of your elk, will you bring them guidance? The fire will come, like Margaret dreamed. They won't be together anymore, and they won't have each other to share our teachings and our dreaming. You will be the only one. Do they hear you? Do they accept you?"

Trudy closed her eyes and looked the wolves in the eye. "I am a true teacher of spirit. I will give them the biggest gift of all. I will open the gate for them to look in and see their god. Ah, dear sacred wolves, eh, my sacred elk, is this so? The essence of your spirits in our lives brings us to a place where we feel the Great Spirit's presence here in our everyday and in our bodies. I will give this gift to the girls, and they will become warriors for the light. Their enlightenment will enhance others; their journey will be a map for others to walk."

Then Trudy opened her eyes and stood up. She saw the wolves listening to her intently. She saw them absorbing her energy and processing her message.

Nala felt a sadness suddenly. "These girls, they live now without the bliss of the Great Spirit inside. We see and feel its presence in them, but we have not given them the bridge yet. As we prepare them for their journeys, this is most important."

Trudy realized that Nala wasn't wasting any time; she had gone straight into ceremony. Nala had no concept of time; the idea was planted, and she was creating the reality.

She moved into the center of their setting and called in many beings. Her howls were cranking, with jolts and starts forming a heartbeat rhythm and resonating infinitely. In time, the beings came; the archangels first all stood in a row, then the winged ones and the four-legged spirits. The water beings created waterways and swam upstream to the meeting point. There was a chorus of angelic voices coming from the sky, and the star nations' light shone on them.

Nano turned to Trudy and said, "Bring in the girls." His eyes and forehead were stern, deepening his voice.

Trudy sent out her feelers and brought the girls into the circle. In their dreambodies, they stood rubbing their eyes, warm enough in their bare feet, and looked each other over with their dreaming eyes.

"We're dreaming, right?" Hanna asked Trudy, who she could see very clearly. She wasn't quite sure where she was, if this were a dream or if she were awake. She knew she'd been in bed and must have fallen asleep because that was where her memory stopped. What followed were more sensations than thoughts, and now she was here in her nightgown with no shoes on, but so was Margaret and that made it okay. She knew the wolves were with them. She couldn't see them, but she heard their breath and felt fur on her cheek a bit.

Margaret was frozen in her spot next to a big boulder, which she leaned back on. From this perspective, she could see everything but kept a firm grasp to the large stone as if it were an anchor, bringing gravity and sensation in her body.

Hanna moved over to Margaret easily. She could see Margaret was stuck and tried to loosen her up by joking. "What ya think, Mar? Can we walk through all these beings, or do you think you could go up and touch one?"

Margaret engaged and managed a smile. "You first. If you can touch Trudy right now, I'll try and touch the wolf."

"I think I'm just gonna walk straight through her." Hanna proceeded forward toward Trudy, who was watching them; she made herself almost invisible by pulling in all of her energy and held her breath.

Hanna reached her with a few steps and stretched out her arm with a pointed finger, feeling out the beyond. Trudy snickered, trying to stay silent. Hanna looked intently into Trudy's eyes as she moved her finger closer and closer to her shoulder until she felt a deeply heated feeling in her gut. Her finger felt nothing as it waved in and through Trudy's shoulder.

Hanna ran back to Margaret, who'd been watching with a large grin on her face; it faded when Hanna came back and said, "Okay, now your turn!"

Margaret looked over at Trudy, who hushed them and motioned for them to sit down and stay in their place. It must have been a feeling she projected, because Margaret could hear no words or voices coming from her, only the harmonic chant of angels.

Hanna and Margaret huddled together and very quickly became aware of the anticipation in the air. Something huge was about to occur, and the girls had no concept of what; they only knew in their gut to pay attention and not play about.

Nano trotted over to the two girls and circled them. Then he sat down opposite them and began to dig a hole in the ground. The soil was flying all over, and the girls moved back out of the way.

Nano jumped out of the hole and suddenly said in clear language, "You see this hole? You see what came out? You have to empty out all the soil, and it flew all over you and got stuck in your eyes, and you are shaking it out now and it will fall to the earth and fill in the hole I just dug. You see? It's all a circle. And we are part of that circle, and we want you to feel your god on earth. Your god on earth is the spirit that fuels your life force. It is the energy that jumps you up out of bed in the morning with joy and excitement in your heart. It is the love and the trust that you allow yourself. Have either of you asked yourself the question yet? Where does God come into all of these things we've shown you?"

Nala moved to the center of the circle that they had created. Her silver white coat shimmered in the moon, and each time she moved, they felt an echo of sound. She circled and conjured with all of her might. She would be giving Margaret the answers very soon now, and this was not an easy task for her. She gave, with many misgivings that should have been left behind long ago, yet they remained. Her resistance to give, her withholding of herself from herself, was staring her in the eye. She felt Margaret's presence and the love she had for her; it filled her spirit heart, the darkness and confusion melted away, and Nala approached Margaret, surrounded with loving light. Margaret welcomed and received her Nala, and her body danced the wolf dance as Hanna watched, hypnotized by the scene.

Trudy and Nano sat in sacred witness for a spell. Hanna was aware of Nano next to Trudy but knew she was to observe the dance playing out before them. There was a merging of the body and spirit between Margaret and her spirit wolf. The colors and sounds seemed overwhelming to Hanna initially, who was not accustomed to such dreams. In all, the girls felt a floating sensation, of merely witnessing, though fully participating. Their brains unable to fathom, they reverted instinctively to their hearts and their bellies. It felt good there, and somehow their ego minds allowed the dream to continue.

Eventually, Margaret and Nala settled on the ground and faced each other. Trudy moved forward and joined them. Hanna stood behind and watched her wolf, still settled in the background, half snoozing, disinterested; she understood this to mean for her to pay attention to her surroundings, where Margaret and Nala were facing off on all levels. She only allowed herself to peek for varying moments, shielded, as you would watch an eclipse. The light was deafeningly bright, the message so simple. The message was of acceptance, of true love that bridges us with God. Hanna looked over at her Nano. He nodded to her in agreement; he seemed to be smiling.

Margaret's dreambody was uncomfortable sitting on the ground, and she kept shifting from leg to leg, eventually settling on both, kneeling close to the ground. She was so full of love for her wolf she hardly felt herself as they merged in a separate reality. Nala showed Margaret the future; she showed her as a mother and as a friend and lover. She showed her new and different places and then gave her another verse of the wolf song:

> The rushes move, shifting us forward,
> And we watch for the opening between the lines
> That define and outline the merging of the few
> Truths that lie in us as one.
>
> The truth that we are one, of wolf and girl;
> That peace on earth is of our oneness and
> Challenges us at every gate; that love of self
> Often elusive, is the key to our brightness of light.

Margaret smiled as she listened to the song; she longed for her jump rope and for the playground and for Hanna to be with her in the physical and not the dream. She wanted to wake up, which would have been very disruptive.

Nano got up and walked over to Margaret, brushing his body next to her. She patted him and nuzzled her face on his back; he smelled of cedar, and she inhaled his essence and courage. She turned to her Nala and embraced her and rolled over on her back and let her wolf lick her face. She laughed in delight and jumped up and chased her wolf round in circles, squealing and howling.

The hysteria was maddening to Hanna, and she hid her face in Nano's coat. She wondered why everything was so crazy.

Nano read Hanna's fears and gave her a nudge. She heard him say, "Look, Hanna, look at your future; see where you will go and not. Feel what it's like to grow old and wiser. Just for a moment, get the sensation, so you will remember some day, after they have driven me from you and made you an adult."

"No, wolf, no one will ever convince me you are not real. You are my path to God, and now I know that I will never give it away. Thank you, dear wolf and Nala."

Trudy started drumming, and the two girls sang in tones they knew not; yet their tune was heard by all the heavens as it reverberated infinitely into space.

The sun began to rise on mother earth, and soon it would be time for the girls to wake up in their beds. Trudy and the wolves knew they had to close their dreamtime circle and send the girls home. None of them had done this before, and they were slightly anxious about how they should return and what they should remember and where they would take their new dreaming abilities.

Trudy said, "Let me lead them each to their homes; you two stay here. I'll get them back safe." She did not wait for a response from the wolves, simply eliminated them from her dream, and led Margaret and Hanna by the hand. She pulled Margaret up from the ground and grabbed Hanna as she circled round. "Come now, ladies of light," she said and smiled. "Back to your beds," she sang.

One by one, they followed her blindly, with smiles on their faces.

Hanna awoke suddenly with a deep itch in her heart. She scratched, knowing it wouldn't help, tried coughing, and then she realized there was something in her bed. It was a flower that she'd picked, and its prickers were stabbing her belly. Hanna sat up in bed and examined the flower. She'd seen nothing like it, but just looking at it made her feel a surge of joy from within. It was unexplainable how she had this flower; she didn't much care—it made her happy!

It was Saturday, and there was no school; there were chores around the house to do, but that wouldn't take long, she thought. Then she'd have the rest of the day to go find Margaret and see if she'd had the same dream last night. Suddenly being around the house seemed mundane and boring; she wanted to go out, even though she knew that breakfast and chores came first.

"Don't you want to get washed, Hanna?" her mother asked.

"Well, Mom, I'll get washed up after I've done my chores; don't worry."

Hanna stuffed two quarters of her toast in her mouth and wolfed down her orange juice; then she stood with hands on hips in front of her chores schedule, which hung behind her. "Dust mop the whole upstairs and dust the staircase. Then dust the downstairs living room, including all windowsills. She thought, *wow, that's a lot; it's gonna take me all morning*.

Hanna set to work and soon felt that she had a new energy inside her. Everything seemed to flow. Even her cleaning was fun. She made up a song to sing while dusting, and her chores were immaculately completed! *Hmm*, she thought, *strange; usually something happens in the middle and I get distracted, and it takes ages to get anything done!*

Hanna was intent on getting out the door and simply didn't question her new energy. Once her chores were complete and checked by Mom, she was free to go out.

Margaret woke up feeling very lazy and sleepy. She didn't want to get up, even when her mother came in and pulled at her covers. "Mom," Margaret squawked, "I don't want to get up. I want to sleep all day, Mom. Leave me alone!"

"Come on, Mar!" Her mother gave another pull on the covers. "It's Saturday! We're going to the Farmers' Market. Up you go!"

Margaret dragged herself up and went into her closet to find some clothes. It was nearing summer, and shorts and a tee would be warm enough after the fog lifted. The weather was never predictable, and she knew to dress with layers. Mom had brought her up some OJ, and she slurped on that, still pulling herself out of her own fog. That dream—she suddenly remembered! *Whoa*, she thought… and wondered if Hanna had had the same dream. "I gotta find her today," she thought out loud.

"What was that?" her mother asked.

"Oh nuthin', Mom. I was just saying I want to play with Hanna today. See if we can improve our double jump roping for the competition next week," she lied. Margaret wondered why she'd just lied and not told her mom about the dream last night. About Trudy, about the wolves, and about *God*! Wow, she remembered it all. "Mom, can we go by the playground on our way home from the market? Maybe she'll be there."

"Mar, why don't you just call her?"

"Oh, I don't know. Last time I called, remember, her father? Maybe he will answer again. I don't want to. We can just go to the playground; she'll be there, I know. It's our meeting place."

Then Margaret remembered Trudy's house. *Maybe Hanna will go there*, she thought. *It doesn't matter; I'll check both.*

Trudy Goodenough was scurrying about her small cottage, clearing away the clutter and trying to create a good teaching room for the girls. She knew there would be days when they'd sit inside, and Trudy's house was not set up presently for guests. All of her life had led her to this gift of two apprentices. She wasn't prepared but knew in her heart that it didn't matter. Nothing seemed to matter after the wonderful dream last night. They were all walking around in seventh heaven; however, Trudy continued to invade her house with the duster and scrubbing brush. She could feel in her bones that the girls would soon be arriving. And right she was, as she heard their voices streaming in from the outside.

With total ease, they had met simultaneously at the playground and headed directly to Trudy's cottage on the corner that wasn't always there.

"So, Margaret, explain one thing to me… Now that we've found our bridge to God, what exactly are we supposed to do with it? I mean, it's nice and all, but there must be something we are supposed to be doing, don't you think?" Hanna lamented. She was extremely excited and Margaret was so slow, she tried to wake her up with questions. "Mar?"

"Yeah, Hanna, I'm just waiting till we get to Trudy's, see what she says. I don't know; I'm feeling not all here. I knew I had to get to you, but now I'm not sure. Well, here's Trudy's—lovely woman. Let's go in!" Margaret tugged at Hanna's sleeve.

Hanna let herself be led, and they both arrived chattering like a couple of hens all revved up 'cause the rooster's been.

"Well, well, look at you two, all chummy and like real sisters!" Trudy cleared some space for them to sit in the kitchen while she prepared tea and crumpets. The batter had been made the night before and was cool and ready for baking. Trudy's oven was hot, and she dropped the batter onto an old darkened baking tin, which had baked many a crumpet. The girls took a whiff of the hot oven, and their taste buds watered at the thought.

"You see how your senses are already extra-sensitive this morning? You can smell the crumpets before they are baked!" Trudy laughed, and the girls nodded, with wide eyes following her around the kitchen as she busied herself. "Sit, sit," she repeated. Just rest yourselves, Hanna, Margaret." She stared at both of them, and they understood she meant it.

After a while, once the two had settled, Trudy sat down too. The crumpets would soon be ready, and the tea was brewed. She poured a cup for each of them and left the teapot in the center of the round table.

Hanna looked around her; this kitchen was so different from hers at home. It had a table and a sink and food and all that, but it smelled different; it felt warm inside. Her kitchen was not always safe with Dad around, but here she knew she could enjoy herself and relax. This room was all stone, just like it was outside—no real walls, just round stones, each one a slightly different shade of gray or silver or brown. She counted them and then looked to the floor, where she found wooden floorboards covered with thin parts of cowhide or maybe elk or buffalo. She could see the wooden planks and hear them creak under the hides.

Why didn't Trudy have linoleum, like theirs at home, on her floor? Trudy answered her question inside; she could hear her... "Hanna, it doesn't matter. Our floors are different to give you perspective. See what is important to dwell on and what is not."

"Thank you, ma'am," she said quietly, thinking loudly, *she just read my thoughts! And I just answered her! Ugh, I feel sick, or maybe just dizzy.*

A bell chimed, and Trudy rose to take the crumpets out of the oven. She said, "Let's give them some time to cool, and while we are waiting, I'd like to teach you a prayer that will serve you for many years to come. Come, gather in, my dears." She beckoned Hanna and Margaret close in...

The three sat in a circle, so close their knees touched. Trudy began to sing a verse she had sung her entire life. It was so familiar to her, it flowed out without effort or consciousness, simply flowed from spirit and out of her throat. The sound was heavenly; they could not understand the words. The language sounded familiar, but the words were not decipherable.

Then Trudy began to translate: "This is how we call each other in the dreamtime, haaaaayoooooooolaaaaaa, haoooolaaa." She looked at the girls and said, "and you answer back with your voice of truth. Just let it out however you feel; voice it with tone and rhythm and worry not about the words. And now express your gratitude for these wonderful crumpets by letting me hear your voice! Aaaaaaalaaaaaaa!" She let out her voice in perfect pitch.

Margaret suddenly cried out, "Aaaaaaaa, I'm staaaarrrvvving! Can I pleeeeeease have a crumpet?"

The three of them burst out laughing, and Trudy stretched over to the counter for the crumpets. They each had a plate with butter and jam. Hanna held her teacup up with a toast. "Tea is good!" she called as she buttered her crumpet and dunked it in her tea; then she popped it into her mouth and with crumpeted mouth muffled, she said, "This is so good!… Trudy, we both had dreams with you last night. The wolves were there, too, and we woke up feeling different. It's hard to say how, but we know we are different, and we want to know what to do now."

"I understand," Trudy said solemnly. Her eyes were sparkling in the sunshine streaming in through the open front door. "Ah, see it's warmer now; sun's come! Let's sit in the garden." She stood and patted the girls' shoulders, picking up the pan of crumpets and teapot in the same hand and gently ushering them out the door.

Once they were sitting again and comfortable, Margaret said, "Ma'am, I see we are here to learn. I have lessons that my wolf wants me to learn, and I think they are about things for later in life when I'm more grown-up. I don't know why this is different and why this isn't something scary. Maybe our cat would!" She laughed and looked to Trudy for an answer. "Trudy, what's this all about? And what's going to happen with us? We can't go on having nights of dreams like last night without someone at home finding us missing."

"I understand, Margaret. Last night was very unusual, and important. We needed to all meet and feel each other on another level in our dreams. It was very successful. You should both be very pleased with yourselves. You did very well. Sometimes we just have to quicken things a bit to bring you up to speed. We have so much to teach you and not very much time…"

"What do you mean, not much time?" Hanna interrupted. "Where are you going?"

"The question is not where am I going, as I am staying here; the question is, where are you going? You are both so young and have such lifetimes ahead! Our meeting will soon be a slight memory from when you were ten years old; imagine that." Trudy was looking very intently at them.

The girls thought and looked at each other; they had never imagined themselves in any other place but where they were. They couldn't imagine what such a memory would feel like.

Trudy continued, "That's why we are giving you so much now, so you remember it well. Let this be one of your most vivid memories, and you will never doubt the power of yourself and your god."

Trudy took Hanna's hand and looked at her intently. "Hanna, when we hold hands, feel the exchange between us."

Trudy then touched Margaret's hand; she jumped slightly, and Trudy gently smoothed the top of her hand and watched her. Margaret looked up at Trudy and smiled invitingly; Trudy's eyes eased from her and she held Margaret's hand close to her heart. "Oh Margaret, young one who has so many journeys ahead of her! Is that what we shall call you?" She laughed.

Tears leaked from Margaret's eyes as she took Trudy's hand in hers and kissed it. "Thank you, Trudy, truly with all my heart, thank you. Suddenly I feel at peace. Like it's good… Hanna, did you receive your lessons from your wolf? Do you know what's coming?"

"Well, Margaret," Hanna began, "last night, I was guided to watch you. I kept looking to my wolf, and he wasn't too interested and urged me to watch the dance between you and Nala. It was so beautiful! My wolf is restful. I'm not sure if I received all my lesson."

Trudy leaned in between them while munching on her second crumpet. "Hanna, your life on earth is so different from Margaret's. I want to say you will have an easier time, because your spirit is at peace with itself, but here, with your family, there is struggle. There is fear. I feel this; there is danger from your father. I know this. Hanna, you have the self-love inside you from spirit, your god, to survive him. Your lessons in this life will be very physical, Hanna; for Margaret the lessons will be different, on another level. She is working with her spirit self and her spirit body. You have already learned this lesson, and you can help her with it."

"How do you mean?" Hanna asked.

"Give her your peace, young one. Give her the soft pillow to rest her head on and feel safe. This is what you can give Margaret."

"Thank you, Trudy." Hanna bowed her head. She didn't really understand, but she knew it meant that Margaret needed her.

"Hanna, thank you for being my friend and twin sister," Margaret said, looking Hanna in the eye and speaking from her heart. She had tears in her eyes, her joy showing on her creased-up smiling face.

Trudy watched them intently and felt the sadness again when she knew they would be separated soon. Their spirits were intertwined, and the physical separation would be a strain on all. They all knew that this process was part of each of their journeys; even Hanna and Margaret, as young as they were, understood.

Hanna said, "You know, Margaret, I need help from you too. You don't have a dad at home, but I do. I don't know if all dads are like him, but he's scary some of the time, and other times he's so great. But I don't know if he's going to be nice or not, so I never feel good with him. He makes me count—I know it. He's the one I'm afraid of when I go home every day, not knowing what he will be like as I arrive at home, so it makes me count, and somehow it gets me up the path and in the house. Most times he's okay, but like last week, he smacked me, and it was so scary I ran out of the house and hid in the backyard. My mom told me to run!"

Trudy stroked Hanna as she spoke. She could feel her fear dissipating as she released what had happened that evening upstairs in their bedroom. Trudy was able to see events occur as they happened sometimes; she was watching the scene as Hanna described it. She held her anger inside and knew she could release it on Hanna's father someday. She saw herself scolding him, and then corrected herself—no, not scolding, reprimanding him! The feeling was very close.

As she questioned her sudden strong feelings, the sky seemed to cloud over, and an eerie feeling was present. The three turned to the street beyond Trudy's tall shrubs and heard loud footsteps and the sound of a man ranting. Jay was approaching them, his arms waving in the air, his step aggressive, and every swear word Hanna had ever heard was spewing out of him. He grabbed Hanna by the arm when he arrived and yanked her out of her chair up to her feet.

"Daaaad," Hanna protested, only to be shaken again by his powerful arm. She quieted and looked to Trudy pleadingly.

Trudy acknowledged her by softly closing her eyes for a moment, and then she looked up directly to Jay and said, "Come, sir, come and join us. We were just speaking of you, sir. Will you, please?" Trudy stood up and offered Jay her seat.

He looked over to Trudy and dropped Hanna's arm. Feeling squeamish suddenly, he slipped into her chair and sat quietly. It was as if Trudy had waved a magic wand over him and completely transformed his rage.

Hanna was amazed and smiled.

Dad saw it and said, "So, introduce me to your friends, Hanna. What are you doing here?"

"How did you find us, Dad? We only just discovered this house, and we liked the garden and the lady let us come and sit with her. She has crumpets, Dad. Want one?"

"I am Margaret, sir. I called Hanna once," she said meekly, hoping he wouldn't roar at her again.

Jay stared at her for a moment, but Trudy interrupted by offering him tea and crumpets. The plate had two freshly buttered ones, cut in half, and his tea was poured. Jay tucked into the food and tea, ignoring Margaret.

"Yes, Mr....?" Trudy began.

"Templeton," he said, "Jay Templeton." As he offered her his handshake and stood halfway, he asked, "And you are...?"

"Trudy Goodenough, retired grandmother. How do you do, Jay? Your daughter, Hanna, has a green thumb and has been full of questions about my garden. What a joy to share with such a young'un. Don't you agree?"

Jay looked at Trudy's garden and did not recognize any of the plants, nor did he care. He was surprised to hear that it interested Hanna and was suspicious. He glanced over to his daughter and said, "So, Hanna, what have you learned here? What's the name of this plant, and why would this grandmother be growing it?"

Hanna looked at Trudy.

"Don't look at Trudy; look at me!" Jay nearly raised his voice, his eyebrows jumping up and down with his words.

"Um, that one there?" Hanna asked, stalling, hoping for something to say. She had no idea what that was, and Trudy and she had never discussed the garden!

"Um, Trudy, didn't you say you made tea with that plant?"

Trudy smiled and agreed. "Oh, yes, it's called Luisa. I never told you the name, but yes, that is the one you picked for our tea. Margaret, go and fetch me some dried sage; we will burn it here and cleanse the air—if that's okay with you, Jay?"

She turned to him, and he nodded but didn't understand what she meant. "Burn, did you say? I don't see any pit here for burning, or a BBQ. Where would you burn anything here?"

"See, Jay, in here, this beautiful abalone shell, it can hold a sprig of sage for the burning. It's not a bonfire we are starting here," she said curtly.

There was tension between the two; Trudy was trying with all of her power to keep it friendly. For the girls' sake, for the future; because Hanna's future with her depended on this meeting with her father. It was good for Trudy to meet him personally and feel his energy and experience him. Trudy was acknowledging her gratitude for this gift, however warped. The friction between them would remain, but she could conjure the energies so as not to make it hostile. He was controllable; he was very susceptible to her feminine nurturing energy, and she would charm him with it. *Templeton*, she thought, *interesting name*.

Jay was sitting in Trudy's chair; Trudy was perched on the edge of the table opposite him as he sipped the tea and munched the crumpets. "A very good crumpet, you make, ma'am, thank you." Jay's gentler side had returned; the tea's attributes had calmed his fear.

Margaret returned from the other side of the house, where she had found the white sage bundles that Trudy had put together and hung in the shed. She'd sniffed them earlier during their first visit, and Trudy had told her about the sage and its uses. She handed it over to Trudy, who trimmed it up and lit a match, which she had pulled from her apron pocket.

The sage leaves flared up from the match, and Trudy let the flame burn for a few seconds and then blew it out, causing a stream of smoke to curl up before her. She smiled and breathed in the smoke like she was smelling a sweet rose.

Jay watched the ceremony and began to twitch his nose at the new aroma in the air.

Trudy noted his discomfort and said, "Jay, just ignore the smoke as you would a room deodorizer; it just cleans the air."

"I understand that. What I don't understand is why you would use it outdoors. Maybe even at night against mosquitoes, I could understand, but in the clear daylight, outdoors?"

"Oh, but it does help keep the flies and the bees away; keeps them off the food, Jay."

"Hmmmm," he noted.

Trudy said, "I know, let's have a game of cards. I'm sure I have a deck in the house. Shall I go look?"

"I don't want to play cards, Trudy; we are here to learn. Dad, you want to sit in on our lessons about the garden, or what would you like to do?" Hanna said, feeling she really didn't want him there.

The wolves could feel the tension in the air. They felt an explosion coming and knew that they could only witness. They fed their girls with as much light and courage as they could muster.

"Enough!" Jay slammed his fist on the table, and everything clattered. "What's this stupid idea, playing a game of cards, madam? Who are you, and what are you doing with my daughter? Do you think you could distract me with a game of cards? Me, a high-powered attorney in the city? You really think you could slither past me? So, my daughter says you have something to teach her, so spit it out. What is your motive with my girl?"

Trudy wanted to grab the girls and run. It was her first instinct, but she knew better. She knew she was a powerful woman of spirit and she could somehow make this explosion evaporate. "Well, if you really want to know, Mr. Templeton, or is it Your Honor? How would you like me to address you? I am an expert in vegetable gardens, vegetables we call superfoods, like spinach and kale. I also specialize in herbs that I make into ointments; they are sold in the drugstore. Your daughter has expressed an interest in these herbs; she wants to learn their healing attributes, and that is what I am teaching her. Do you have an objection, sir?"

"Yes, I do. I do because I don't believe you, but I'll get it out of my daughter tonight, if I have to pull her teeth out!"

Trudy shuddered at the thought, and the girls huddled behind her. Hanna was petrified, and Margaret stood shaking next to her. Hanna knew she'd have to reach her mom somehow and not be alone with Dad. He was crazy, she thought. She would never tell him about the wolves, *ever*. She thought of the torture she could endure. No, she still wouldn't tell. *Never*. He would kill them. She knew. She could feel Nano's breath on her back. It was cool and breezed through her hair; she almost lifted her hand to caress his fur but kept her hand down. She felt full of his energy, his courage, his calm, and allowed the words to float from her.

"Oh, Dad, it doesn't matter, it really doesn't. We have a competition at school, and this lady is helping us. Come on; let's all go home, Dad." Hanna's voice was calm and soft; her tones created a love between them. She spoke with affection and gazed at him, pouting. "Come on, Dad." She clutched his hand, and he let her.

Jay felt the heat coming from his daughter; he recognized her loving warmth, and it softened his heart, even though his brain continued to rage. Feeling split, he fell into her loving spell, got up calmly, and nodded at Trudy as if hypnotized. "Good night, ma'am."

That was the last the girls heard from Jay as they said their good nights; then they walked Margaret home. When she was dropped off, Hanna and Jay walked home in silence. The footsteps echoed down the lane, and as they crossed over the stream, Hanna could see how unsteady her dad was. She grabbed his hand in support, and he smiled. She continued to breathe in and out the energy her wolf was sending her. It kept her calm and loving. She didn't even have the urge to count as they approached their home.

Chapter 5

No one would have believed that such violence could roll though the girls' lives the way it did that night. When Jay and Hanna got home, he tore the house to bits, including Hanna, her mom, and Michal. Trudy had sensed what was about to occur and called the police as soon as they had left to warn them. But they only arrived after Jay had done the damage. He was found dancing around the front yard covered in blood and sweat. He had wounded himself, as well as everyone else; a convoy of ambulances lined up and took them all to the hospital.

Trudy had watched as Jay and Hanna walked home quietly the evening before. She knew the man was about to erupt and had taken the necessary precautions, although she trusted that the police would meet him at the house and prevent the massacre. She watched in her mind's eye as his rage erupted when they arrived at home and he began to take it out on the furniture and Hanna. Michal and Carol tried to stop him, but he turned on them as well. All three were found unconscious when the ambulances arrived. It was doubtful who would survive.

Margaret's apartment burned down that night, together with the entire apartment complex. By morning, all that was left were burning embers, ash, and a massive demolition site. Residents wandered around in shock, draped in blankets or anything else they could grab.

Margaret and her mom were waiting to be picked up by Auntie Mags, for whom Margaret had been named. She was ill when Margaret was born, and the story was that Margaret's birth brought her back to health. Margaret adored her auntie. They were going to live at her house in the country, and she would be able to have a dog there. Margaret looked at the ruins of her home and thought about her Nala, hoping that she would join her if she brought home a dog.

It was morning now, and she had to get hold of Hanna. She hoped that Auntie Mags would stop by her house on the way out of town so she could say good-bye. "Do you think she will, Mom?" Margaret pulled at her mother's shirtsleeve, which was torn and dirty. Her mom looked pretty upset, and Margaret sensed this wasn't the time for questions. She would ask Auntie Mags herself. She realized that she'd have to do a lot herself now; her mom didn't look too good.

Eventually Auntie Mags arrived, and they packed up what they could salvage from their apartment into her big car.

Margaret didn't think she'd ever been in a car so big! "Wow, Auntie Mags, you could fit a million people in here!" she said and hugged her as she got in the car. "Mags, can we stop to say good-bye to my friend Hanna? She doesn't live far; I have to see her!"

"Sure, Margaret, just tell me where she lives."

Suddenly Margaret realized that she didn't actually know where Hanna lived. She knew about where, but she didn't know the exact house. She decided that at night she would contact her wolf and hopefully she would pass the word. "That's all right; I don't really know where she lives," Margaret said, slightly embarrassed.

"Do you have her telephone number?" Mags asked.

"Yes, we have that, right, Mom?" Margaret said, looking at her mother, who had her head in her hands, sitting in the front seat of the car.

"I don't know what we have, Margaret; you can look it up in the book," she managed.

"Don't worry, Margaret; we'll find her once we get back home," Mags said, concentrating on the traffic. "Hush now. I have to navigate this city traffic and find my way to the road out of town."

Margaret sat back in her seat and tried to connect with her wolf. She fell asleep instantly and dreamed about the fire. This time the dream was like she already dreamed it, and she almost felt bored. Margaret was in a state of complete surrender. She knew that her wolf would take care of her and knew that all this would happen. She awoke when they arrived at Mags's home.

Margaret peered out of the window to find a stark lone white house standing in the middle of a lot with no grass, a barbed wire fence surrounding it, and absolutely nothing else. The house was covered with white shingles, grayed from years of rainy winters. The area seemed like a desert. Margaret wondered if she could get anything to grow here, and her mind drifted off to Trudy's magnificent garden.

The wolves watched intently from above. The two balanced on a tree branch, both sitting quietly and witnessing the events. They must build strength and character, and this journey of disaster in the physical provided the girls with endurance to survive and thrive. They protected Hanna's life, as Jay would have murdered her, but more than that was not allowed. Margaret's life was never in danger. The fire began at the other end of the complex, which gave Margaret and her mother the chance to load up some belongings and get out. The wolves pushed and pulled the energies so that there were no deaths, but the structure was lost.

They watched as Margaret explored her new home and knew that they would need a separate time alone with Hanna. She would need much support, and they needed to find a way for Trudy to visit her. Hanna was still unconscious. She would dream on for a day, and this was a gift, enabling Trudy to be at her side when she did awake.

Trudy had surrounded herself with her sacred objects and candles; she was chanting and burning sweet grass, cajoling with the spirit world and praying for Hanna and Margaret. Her energies drew in the wolves, and they lay down on her wooden floor next to the table where she sat.

Nano licked her boot and nudged it slightly from the floor. He said, "Aye, woman, you must visit my girl, wake her up, tell her, be with her, tell her."

Trudy responded, "I suppose her grandmother or some relative will come to take her, wolf. I'm sure she has some family."

"No family, Trudy," he said. "They were here alone; that's why I chose them. You will be Hanna's only family now. Except for Margaret, her girl. Where is she? Fire, I saw; she leaves, too."

Nano nosed Nala, who was snoozing. "What you do with your girl?"

"She's okay," Nala answered. "She don't need me now. Look what we did. We got Jay all angry, and look where fear took him. We need to stay out of their lives; it's too dangerous. Trudy, you take Hanna. Bring her up good, but keep them grounded. We will visit them another time, another place, and we will make it so."

"I don't understand you, Nala," Trudy complained. "You come and totally take over her life, and then you just abandon her? This is when she needs you most. She's alone, separated from her friend, and soon she'll find out how sick she is. She needs your love and strength. She needs to know you are behind her. She will fall without you." Trudy was standing in the middle of the room, waving her arms and making a scene.

Nano interjected with a long yawn and said, "We cannot abandon them. We must go to them in the dreamtime and give them what they need. We must bring the two girls together once last time for now. Remember the promises? Remember what we decided about the promises? And now we have another verse to sing the girls, and we must go and do that!" Nano said gruffly and began to dig at the ground, ready to take flight. "Come on!"

The three surfaced at the hospital in Hanna's room. She lay in bed peacefully, her bed and her surroundings untouched by visitors, starkly sterile, with no personal effects. Trudy materialized with a bouquet of flowers and a teddy bear in her arms. She placed the flowers down and tucked the teddy bear under Hanna's covers next to her. She was so peaceful. Trudy glided her hand over her cheek; it was cool, and Trudy felt warmth within her travel down her arm into her hand and straight into Hanna's heart. There was clear passage, and Trudy was comforted, knowing that Hanna would soon be awake and with them again.

Hanna could feel a presence and wondered where she was. She was afraid to move and preferred the darkness of her eyes closed, so she wouldn't know where the next blow would come from. She could only feel comfort inside; she didn't know where Dad was. This created a fear within, and it was paralyzing. Trudy took out a fan from her bag and waved it over Hanna.

The wolves were perched up above. They opened the skies and let the chorus of angels into the room. Their voices enveped Hanna and caressed her with tones and harmonics of clarity and calm. Hanna soon began to feel her toes and her knees and her belly. Blood began to circulate around her belly and heart, and she soon felt flushed on her face and itchy. Her body reacted first; she remained asleep as she began to scratch herself.

Trudy waved her fan over Hanna's belly and then put it away in her bag before the nurse came in. Hanna's eyes began to flutter, and Trudy knew she wouldn't have much time. "Hanna, my child," she whispered in her ear. "Do you hear me? Smile if you hear me; don't wake up just yet." She continued, holding Hanna's hand, "Squeeze my hand if you hear me, child." Hanna felt a sudden joy emerge from within, an excitement that made her want to explode. She squeezed Trudy's hand.

"Okay, now, listen. We haven't much time. Your mother and Michal have passed over, and I am going to fix it so you can come and live with me. Margaret's house burned down last night, and she has moved with her mom out of town. We will connect with her when you come home. You are in the hospital; you are going to get better. I love you, Hanna."

The tight squeeze of Hanna's hand loosened with every word she heard. Tears erupted from her eyes like little irrigation pipes when you turn the water on, eventually drowning her cheeks… She awoke to wipe her eyes and sat up, staring horrified at Trudy. "Where's Dad?"

"They put him away, Hanna. Don't worry; he'll never hurt you again."

"He killed Mom and Michal? What about Trixie? Where's Trixie? Where's Lovely?"

"We'll find them, Hanna. They are fine, at the house. I will pick them up and take them home today, okay?"

"Okay," Hanna said and rested back on her pillow. "My head hurts. My jaw hurts. My legs hurt. Trudy?"

"Yes, child, you are seriously injured in all your body. You are young and strong, though, and you will heal. You will have a good life."

Hanna started to cry. "Mooooooom, my brother Mikey! Oh my God! I don't believe it! Daaaaaad, why? Trudy, was it my fault? I don't remember what happened. What happened?"

The nurse came into Hanna's room, and Trudy sat back and smiled at her with all of the love and care of a nurturing nursemaid. "Good day to you, good nurse. Look who has come back to us."

The nurse wasn't as cordial. "I don't believe I've met you, ma'am. You are…?"

A Wolf Song

"Oh, I'm sorry for not introducing myself, nurse. Trudy Goodenough; I'm the girl's Godmother. I came in the middle of the night, and you were all busy; I didn't want to bother you. I've been looking over her for a few hours now."

The nurse grabbed Hanna's chart and studied it. "I don't see any notes here about a godmother."

Trudy said, "Does it say anything about the mother or the brother?"

The nurse checked. "No, it only says it's a 'domestic.' I try and stay away from those. Here, let me get another nurse; she's more specialized in these cases. And you," she said, looking Trudy in the eyes, "you have to get yourself registered. Come with me."

Trudy got up from her chair and looked reassuringly down to Hanna, patting her on the shoulder. "Be right back, child."

They left the room, and Hanna closed her eyes again. Her thoughts were full of questions, and she looked up to the stars in her imagination and saw her wolf standing there, looking at her with pride. She saw his pride and filled with joy. She looked to him and asked, "Are Mom and my brother all right, wolf? Where are they now? Can I talk to them in my dreams, wolf? I want them to know I'm okay. Wolf? Are they okay?"

"Your mother and brother are full of light and love now, Hanna. They travel in spirit with you always."

"What does that mean, wolf? Like when I'm dreaming? Exactly when are they with me?"

"They are with you always. You can feel them on your cheek; you can feel their love in your heart. That is their new presence in your life. You will always feel them. You must decide if this will give you strength, or if it will weaken you and destroy you from melancholy."

"What's melancholy?"

"Melancholy is deep sadness. It can be so deep that it makes you sick," Nano said.

Hanna woke up from her dream and was thankful knowing that Nano was close by. Trudy and another nurse soon came in. Somehow Trudy had gained their confidence. There was talk of police interviews and social workers. Hanna knew this had to do with her mother's death. She felt numb. She kept wondering what she was supposed to feel; she kept wanting to talk to Margaret.

She had an idea. Maybe they could call Margaret on the telephone. A new feeling of happiness, the first she'd felt since waking, was circulating inside. She felt like getting up and getting dressed.

The nurse pushed her playfully back down and said not yet, but maybe she could try and walk after dinner and have a bath.

"Trudy! Can we call Margaret?" Hanna asked, all excited.

"Hanna, we'll have to do some research and find her telephone number. She must have left town a couple of days ago when her house burned down. I told you—don't you remember?" "What?" Hanna remembered Trudy talking about it, but she'd forgotten with all of the other news.

"Oh yeah," she acknowledged. "So, how are we going to find her?"

"Trust, my child." Trudy stretched her arm over Hanna and embraced her. "You must trust that everything is going to be all right." Trudy rocked her.

Hanna closed her eyes and tried with all her might to imagine her and Margaret jumping rope in the playground near both of their homes. She tried and tried to jump rope, up and down, up and down, trying to look into Margaret's eyes. Hanna exhausted herself in her efforts and opened her eyes again.

"Trudy, I can't do it; maybe you can find her for me?"

"When you are well enough, we will find Margaret. Don't you worry about that. I want you to concentrate on getting stronger and walking, you hear, Hanna? Never mind the dreams right now. I want you to make your body strong again. You need to rest. Maybe I should go and come back tomorrow?"

"Oh no, Trudy, don't go!" Hanna protested.

"Well, I can't stay here overnight, Hanna, but I can stay all day if you wish."

"Oh yes, please. I promise I'll go to sleep if you stay!"

Trudy sat down in the chair next to the bed and pulled out some beading she was working on. She sat back and went into a silence, which allowed Hanna to fall asleep. They sat the rest of the day in this state: Hanna healing, Trudy contemplating her new role in life with Hanna. The quiet nourished them both; the silence filled them with peace. It was the exact prescription Trudy had asked for.

Jay Templeton was incarcerated in the city jail awaiting transportation to the psych ward, where he would be assessed. Under observation already, he swung at the cameras installed above him on the walls and ceiling of his cell. He ranted to them and then begged their forgiveness; he admitted guilt and then backed out, providing alibi after alibi and stating that he hadn't beaten and killed his family, but it was a home intrusion and he walked in on them. Then would cry again with guilt and disgust of himself. "Why didn't you let me die?" he asked the empty stone walls.

A guard passed by and looked in to make sure he hadn't hung himself yet. They wanted him to stand trial; they wanted to see him punished.... Killed his family—such a monster. Jay Templeton was a condemned man; there would be no mercy.

How he prayed for a moment with that old woman now. He knew she could help, but he didn't know how he could reach her. Trudy felt a tug in her belly as Jay drew her into his hell. She was very impressed with his power and wary of it. This man seemed to perform like a sorcerer who didn't know he was one. He possessed such power of passion, which was misused and targeted in his rages. *If only*, she thought, *he could use his power in rightful ways*. He was clearly living in darkness and wanted to bring everyone else down with him. Trudy wondered if the doctors and the court would consider him sane.

He was wearing a jail jumpsuit over his blood-caked clothes, which the police had neglected to remove. His hair was matted, and he thought about his phone call. They hadn't let him make a phone call yet, and he had to call his office to cancel his appointments. He wondered if his firm would defend him. He'd blocked out the night before and wasn't sure why he was there—but then he remembered again: he'd killed his family. The memory seemed to weave in and out of his consciousness. They hadn't told him that Hanna had awakened, and he assumed they were all dead.

"So," he cried and stood banging and hanging on the bars of his city jail cell. Others shouted back at him to shut up. A flood of cursing followed between cells until a guard came and shouted over the calls, threatening lights out early.

A silence came over the small provincial jail, which was not fitted for murderers. Most of the visitors were drunks and prostitutes rounded up the night before, all trying to sleep off their hangovers. Jay's lunacy was disruptive; they all knew he was different. Even the guards were wary of him, calling for backup at his every whim. When he threw his food all over the cell walls, they watched with intrigue, and then hosed the place down with cold water. Jay was now soaked as well as matted, sweaty, and blood-crusted.

He sat huddled in a corner of the jail cell. His experience with the voices still echoed in his mind, and confusion replaced any clarity he had left. The jail doctor arrived, and guards opened the cell door. Jay sat frozen in a ball in the corner. The doctor asked him how he was, and he did not respond. The doctor rested a hand on his shoulder, and he shuddered and shrank further into the floor. Inside he felt like a ball of poisonous gel, able to shape shift and drool out of the cracks in the walls. He set his mind on this task, which would make him invisible and impossible to detect by the people. The doctor shook his head and told the guards to send him to the county mental hospital under secure guard in a padded cell. This man was clearly suicidal and probably not capable of standing trial. He wrote his assessment, and Jay was formally declared insane.

Trudy kept track of his whereabouts, one of her fiduciary duties. Someday Hanna might wish to see him.

The following day, Margaret woke up at her auntie's. Her mom was still staring at the walls where she sat when they'd gone to bed. She seemed to be in a trance, and Margaret couldn't wake her. Mags tried, too, but could only get her to take a few sips of water.

Margaret was intent on finding Hanna after Mags had made her breakfast and sat down in front of the telephone book. Once she found the telephone number, she asked to use the phone.

Mags offered to make the call; it might be easier if she spoke with Hanna's mom first. Margaret agreed and gave her the number.

Once Mags was connected, her face seemed concerned. After a moment of listening, she slowly put the receiver down and looked up at Margaret with tears in her eyes.

"Auntie Mags, what's happened? What's wrong? Why are you crying, Auntie?"

"I'm not sure yet, lovey. Why don't you go run outside and play for a bit, and Auntie will make some phone calls. I'll see if I can't find Hanna for you."

Mags had listened to a message that was on their machine; it said that the house was a crime scene and any interested parties should call the police. Mags called the number provided and was informed of the circumstances of the crime after many questions. She was very shocked and wasn't sure how she would break the news to Margaret. It was good news that Hanna had survived, and she was grateful she could give Margaret this information; however, Margaret wasn't doing too well, and her mom was even worse.

Mags hoped something good would come from all of this turmoil. It felt like life had just thrown another tornado on them. *Murder? Poor young girl, a victim? And Margaret, so disturbed already?* There was so much to consider, and Mags was not used to being a mother.

She walked over to her sister to check in. Joan was still staring, although she had changed position and was now facing the table looking for food.

"Oh darling, are you hungry? Shall I make us some soup? How would you like some soup, Joan? Will you have some soup and home-baked bread with me?" Mags practically pleaded. She didn't want to tell Margaret what had happened; she hoped her mother would recover and handle it. "Joan, come and sit down. I have something to tell you," Mags said to her.

Joan looked up and turned toward her sister. "What, Mags? What do you want of me? Let me just sit here."

Mags hoped that maybe other people's bad news might spring Joan out of her own misery. "You know Margaret's friend, Hanna?"

"The sweet one, yes, of course. She's all Margaret talks about! What about her? Did Margaret find her and tell her we've moved?"

"Well…" Mags hesitated. "Hanna is in the hospital. Her mother and brother are dead, and her father is in prison. It all happened a couple of days ago, when your house was burning. Don't ya think that's weird? Those two girls are connected with something, you know, Joan. What is it with them? Margaret speaks only of Hanna, Hanna, Hanna!"

Joan smiled. "Yes, they are like sisters, twins in fact, did you know? Born on the same day, those two; same hospital too. They only met recently in the park. Something they have about jumping roped. Yes, we should find Hanna and make sure Margaret gets to see her. Can you do that, Mags? I'm much too exhausted still. I swear, I will get my energy back; I know it. It's been a long week; my house burned down."

The wolves knew what was needed. Their girls needed them. They needed to know that the love of the great life force that was within them was still without them too. They needed to feel the force of the great one. The wolves opened up the gates of the heavenly sounds from the angels and their instruments, and they knew that the words would come for each one of them.

Nano began. His words fell from the stars like tiny spheres of light moving deeper and farther and closer to Margaret and Hanna.

> Oh softly I touch with my paw so dear.
> Those steps I see you take and draw
> Back to me your source.
> I give you a path; walk on it strong.
> Stay there, stay put, and hold on tight.
> There may be movement for our stream together,
> And my journey yet here and now will be watching you
> from afar.

Hanna, lying in her bed, felt the words stream in on fully adorned unicorns. Each one hopped off and filled her heart till it felt it would burst. She watched and caught them and listened and knew. Then she sang:

> Oh wolf, today I give you a verse of your wolf song,
> For you are with me and my heart is full from you.
> In you I see my celebration; in you I feel my graduation.
> You are to me, a second half, a piece dropped off and taken on,
> There for when.
> For whens like this, for whens like now,
> When it's all gone and no one to fare
> And all I see are presents everywhere!
>
> The leaf will flip and be and flopped and be
> And I will be.

Jay knew he was hearing his daughter. The chords were good, and they sounded beautiful and they softened him. He allowed himself to indulge and really listen this time. He heard the words; he heard his girl, singing, celebrating, and alive. Then he heard his own voice from way, way far away. His voice seemed so far away that he wondered if he were alive. He let the thought go as his throat developed a fullness and he could feel his voice too.

"Ahhhyeeeee—there are no words. There is no sane. I know you, and I hear your voices."

He knew he was absolutely crazy and that he should pay no attention whatsoever to anything. Yet he still heard the voices, and this time they were nice.

> I know our life was gone; I know you had a life outside me.
> I gave it to you, or I would have taken it away.
> Your mother, my wife, my son, your brother.
> Oh, death on me, dear daughter. I say forgive, forgive.
> And live and live and live.
>
> I say good-bye and do not come to me.

Hanna cried as she heard her dad's voice. She let herself cry out loud into Trudy's arms. Her body shook and turned. She began to sweat.

Trudy put a cold compress on her forehead and lay her back down to sleep. "Sleep now, child, your dad will be fine. You will be fine." Trudy rocked Hanna's arm and blew on her face. "Sleep, child."

Then her voice could wait no more. Her elk self almost jumped out of the chair and began to circle round the room. She could feel herself bringing up her voice from her stomach. There were no words for her; only chords in G's and C's. She let them out with her vibrant voice and felt the angels harmonizing with her. Trudy must have been the chorus, the chorus to sing again and again in-between these verses of horror and grief, in between the gifts and knowns and far beyond the undids.

As she scanned the skies looking out of the hospital-room window, she saw three stars shining deeply toward her. Tears welled within her as she remembered those three stars and the sky she would look at when she was Hanna's age. In the old country, before they moved and everything changed. And here were Margaret and Hanna, about the same age she was when it all changed for her, moving onto separate paths at such a young age! She had hoped they would have their teens together and would separate for adulthood, but that was not the plan. And here they were all in tune, singing the wolf song, waiting for her call. And here it came:

> Your soft touch
> Comes to me
> In tones of dapple and gray.
> I hear them, so I see them stay,
> As the scale you draw out
> Becomes our way.

Trudy and Elk sang the verse together, and their harmony created vibrations through all of them.

Nala was energized and moved about restlessly. Her fur caused a wind of echoed sound as it shifted and turned from her movement.

> I am Nala. I come
> From above, and my girl Mar
> Is in peril. Let
> Her song be heard throughout
> The universe. Let her
> Be heard and listened
> To and heard again.
>
> This Margaretgirl will
> Grow, and I stand tall behind
> Her. Her journey mine;
> My journey hers. Our
> Spiral endless, committed
> To the light like a
> Bug round a flame. We
> Keep each other whole and
> Split ourselves in half.
>
> We see you on the
> Whole side of the moon, dear one.
> You two will be whole!

A Wolf Song

Margaret was in the backyard when she heard the sounds. At first she thought it was simply the sound of silence, since she'd never been anywhere so quiet. Then the chords sounded familiar, and her joy rose from within, flushing her cheeks when she realized her wolf was singing to her.

Margaret could feel her own grief in Nala's growl —short, a high-pitched yelp. After a few howls, Margaret found her own voice.

At first, all she could do was howl. Then the words came. Her high-pitched voice let out short words, slight sentences.

> I hear you.
> I hear you.
> Wolf, are you here? Do you know where I've been?
> Awaaaaay ho! Awaaaaay ho!

Margaret's peeps were barely audible. She crumbled in her yard and felt tears wetting her knees. She closed her eyes.

Nala dove into her thoughts the moment her eyes closed, and Margaret jumped onto her back. Nala leaped to the sky, and they flew.

"Where are we going?" Margaret asked.

Nala did not respond, but no sooner had Margaret spoken than they began to descend in front of the hospital.

Margaret knew this place from various visits during her younger years. "Why are we at the hospital?" She turned to the wolf, but Nala was gone, and Margaret stood on her own in front of the great red-brick building. She closed her eyes again and found her Nala, who directed her up to where Hanna was lying.

Margaret approached her bed and held Hanna's hand.

Hanna, who was still upset and crying, closed her eyes. She saw Margaret standing there with her. She felt her hand and her tears. They stood and held each other. Hanna noticed she could stand in her dream state.

Margaret looked at Hanna, her face contorted with misery. "Why?" she asked. "Why did this all happen to us? Oh dear Hanna, what will become of us? We have no homes. We lost our lives."

Margaret awoke from her dream, still in back of her Auntie Mags's house. She was alone again. No one had seen her. She knew she would have to make it back to town to find Hanna. She had to find Trudy! She had to find a way!

Margaret just couldn't believe her luck as she walked up the hospital steps the following day. She was practically running, even though she had no idea how she would actually find Hanna in this big place. She thought of calling her Nala to lead her but wasn't too sure if she would act normal or not, and she didn't want to make anyone think she was talking to wolves. Mags had dropped her off, promising to meet her out front at 3:00 p.m., which gave her a few hours.

Again Margaret jumped inside for joy as she remembered the evening before, when she overheard Mags on the telephone arranging to drive into town the next day. Margaret had tugged and pulled at Mags till she got off the phone and asked if she could go with her to find Hanna. She'd had a hard time explaining how she knew she was in the hospital, but Mags didn't really pay attention.

As she reached the top of the steps and walked into the huge front lobby, she saw an information desk and went over to ask where the children were. Her plan was to look in every room until she found Hanna.

The lady on duty asked Margaret if she knew her friend's name, and she told her. "That will be third floor, room forty-four. Hmmm, that's interesting. She has her own room next to intensive care; must be a serious case. Hmmmm. How old are you? Have you come with an adult?"

Margaret remembered the hospital rules from when her mom was there. No one allowed under the age of twelve. "I just turned twelve!" she said. The nurse waved her by. "Thank you very much!" she called as she skipped across the lobby to the elevators.

Pressing the three button in the elevator, Margaret felt like her belly was about to burst. She held her hands to it and beamed a grin from ear to ear. The people in the elevator were staring at her, but she didn't care. She was leaning on the door and burst through the moment it opened at the second floor. She sprang back in, bumping into people.

"Careful, child," she heard. It was a familiar voice, and she looked up to find Trudy coming into the elevator with some drinks and sandwiches in her hands. "Just in time for lunch, you are, Margaret. How very nice to see you!" Trudy said, feeling grief and joy at the same time as she knew the two friends would have to separate today.

"Trudy! How did you know? How is Hanna?"

"How did you know, child?" she responded. "Let's wait until we've sat down with Hanna."

Trudy led Margaret out of the elevator at the third floor and down the corridor to Hanna's room. She wasn't even asked about her age, nor did anyone pay any attention whatsoever.

Hanna was asleep when they arrived at her room… Margaret was shocked to see her condition, and looked at Trudy with her jaw dropped, wide-eyed, questioning, inventorying: a black eye, a bandage around her jaw and over her head, one leg tied up in the air with a big white cast on it, and her arm in a sling.

"It's okay, dear." Trudy held her. "Hanna will heal. She'll be as good as new in a month or two once those bones bind."

Hanna was dreaming with Nano. She was riding on his back through green fields speckled with purple and violet wildflowers, and the wind felt like velvet on her skin. She did not feel any of the pain her body was experiencing. Her heart was full from her wolf, but she was anxious and asking him, "What will become of me, wolf? Who will take care of me? I'm not a grown-up yet, and my family is gone?"

"Trudy will be your guardian, Hanna. She will take care of you."

"And Margaret, where is she? Why hasn't she come to me?"

"She is with you, child. She is with you."

Hanna opened her eyes to his words and saw Margaret's face less than two inches away. Margaret was bending over her bed and blowing on her face.

Hanna's face scrunched from her breath, and she smiled and filled with joy. "Oh Margaret, you came," she said and just lay in her bed, feeling her entire body relaxing and the pain easing. She felt a little more comfortable.

"Hanna, what happened?"

Hanna looked at Trudy. "You tell her, Trudy. I don't want to cry again; it makes my ribs ache."

Trudy told Margaret about Jay and about Hanna's mom and brother and the awful night that followed their visit with Trudy.

Margaret listened intently and cried; she just sat and cried. It was the first time she had cried since the fire.

Hanna watched her and then asked, "Margaret, what has happened with you?"

Trudy responded for her. "Hanna, Margaret's apartment complex burned down the night of your attack. Seems it all happened at the same time. I knew something was wrong and I went to your house, but I was too late; the police and ambulances were already there. Margaret, I knew about the fire, but I also knew you were safe. Now listen, you two, I have something to tell you.

"Our great spirit god has orchestrated our lives to come together and to be apart. The universe above and beyond brought you to your wolves and brought you to me. We all came together now, and we will also be saying good-bye. Do you remember when we were meeting with the wolves, and Margaret, you were told about your difficult journey? Hanna, do you remember that your wolf said you would have an easier life so that you would be able to learn other things?"

Hanna said quietly, not lifting her head, "I have lost my family, Trudy."

"Yes, you have, and it is the most difficult journey you will take. I will guide you and love you and nurture you, but I will never replace your family. I feel your grief and will help you heal, Hanna."

Margaret asked, "How is Hanna going to live with no mother? Maybe she can come and live with us."

"Margaret, that is not in our control. Girls, it is now time for you to go your separate ways. I know this must seem like a shock to you, but you were brought together for a reason, and you are being separated for a reason. Hanna will stay with me, and Margaret, you will go back and live with your mother and your auntie. You will meet again, and when it is time for you to meet again, your wolves will tell you. Keep listening to your wolves when you dream at night."

Hanna and Margaret both stared at Trudy. They could not believe their ears. Separate? What was she talking about? They both thought, *That's impossible!*

Trudy could see the surprise and disdain in their eyes. She put one hand on Hanna and one on Margaret. "We are all connected, dears, but we are also separate. It is time for you to follow different lives, and when you are older, you will meet again. Okay? You must agree to this, girls; you cannot fight it. Your life will be treacherous if you fight it and try to see each other."

Hanna spoke first. "Well, I suppose if you promise we will meet again, Trudy, if you really, really promise, I *might* go along with it."

"How long for?" Margaret butted in.

"Yeah, Trudy, how long?" Hanna agreed.

"Darlings, you will meet every ten years for the rest of your lives."

Auntie Mags had found Hanna's room and came in just as Trudy finished speaking. "Nice to meet you; I'm Mags," she said to Trudy.

Trudy turned to her with tears in her eyes and held Margaret close. "Mags, it is time to take Margaret home; Hanna needs her rest. You will not come back again. The girls will not meet again until they are grown."

Mags looked at her strangely and felt drawn to her eyes. The more she looked, the more she was pulled in and left speechless. Her instinct was to ask why, but something inside of her kept her silent. She nodded at Trudy and took Margaret's hand. "Come on, my Margaret girl, let's go shopping!"

She tugged Margaret slightly, and Margaret pulled back, shouting, "No, not yet!"

Hanna sat up and stretched her free hand out. "Margaret, don't go!"

"I have to!" Margaret's eyes filled with tears and stretched herself toward Hanna while being pulled by Mags.

"I love you!" Margaret called as she was pulled from the room.

Hanna remained seated with stretched-out hand. Trudy could see a golden cord between Hanna and Margaret. She closed her eyes and stretched out with a pair of imaginary scissors and cut the golden cord. As she did so, all three of them let out a long howling cry.

Mags grabbed Margaret's hand tighter and ran from the room.

Hanna fell back in her bed and wept.

Trudy looked up at the wolves.

Nano whispered in her ear, "Ten years. Make sure they meet again in ten years."

Part I

Epilogue

One day a letter arrived addressed to Hanna. Trudy collected it from the mailbox outside of the house and walked slowly back while inspecting the envelope carefully and holding it to her heart. She could feel Margaret's heartbeat within it and examined the handwriting and the address she had used. "The stone house on the corner of Jones and Fulton Avenue." No city, no state, no zip code. She felt grief and anger in her hand. She did not see her name on the envelope; it was clearly only addressed to Hanna.

Trudy considered withholding it from her; she even imagined opening it and reading it. Her belly took a turn to the left with that thought, and she listened. *No*, she thought. Her mind wandered and disbanded to the heavens. She prayed out for her own guides and for Margaret's Nala and received very little information. They all turned their back on her, and she knew that she had to listen to her own intuition: the flip-flop of her stomach and the lack of ease in her heart. She would indeed give the letter to Hanna, but she would sit with her as she read it. *Maybe she will offer to read it aloud.* Trudy trusted that Hanna would share; there was no doubt in her heart about that.

When she entered the house, Hanna was at her desk doing homework. She turned to Trudy and said, "Nano just came to visit, Trudy. He tells me you have something for me."

Trudy let out a long knowing chuckle; her belly reverberated, and Hanna giggled, poking her playfully. "What's so funny?"

Trudy laughed. "Nano has his way," she said and chuckled to herself some more. "Yes, Hanna, I do have something for you." She reached out and put the mail on Hanna's wooden desk. "Why don't you go through the mail today? I suppose you are old enough. Here, let's go through it together." Trudy sat down and pushed the pile toward Hanna.

Hanna felt honored to be given the mail; it was a sign that Trudy thought she was old enough, and she smiled with pride. "Thank you, Trudy!" she said as she dug into the pile. It was mostly advertising and letters that Trudy said could be thrown out. Then she came to the light blue envelope with handwriting on it addressed to her. She stopped and stared wildly as she began to comprehend what it was.

Trudy observed her, feeling very protective of Hanna, and was ready to pounce like a bitch with pups if she felt one drop of pain coming from her. It had been many years since they had seen Margaret, and Hanna very rarely spoke of her. Trudy knew that life was not going well for her and was unsure why she was writing. But Nano had made it plain that Hanna should see her letter, and Trudy would be her safety net.

"Trudy, I'm not sure if I should open the letter. Nano said we had to wait till we were twenty, and there's a few more years till then."

"But he just told you about the letter, Hanna. I am sure he wants you to open it. Don't worry; I am here with you, Hanna. I have an idea—why don't we read it together?"

"Okay, Trudy. How about you read it to me? I feel very excited right now; my belly feels like there's a butterfly nest inside! Go on; you read it!"

Trudy took the envelope in her hand, turned it over, and saw Margaret's return address. She hadn't noticed it before. It read, "Kings County Mental Hospital." Her head sank to her chest, and she shut her eyes tight to stop the tears. A long ache spread through her chest area, and she crossed her arms over herself.

Hanna sprang up and hugged Trudy from behind, leaning on the back of her chair. "Trudy, what is it? What did you read?"

Trudy did not respond but began to carefully open the envelope. She slid her pinky nail under the seal and flawlessly opened both sides. The stationery inside held the county emblem and was typewritten. She glanced down to the bottom of the page and saw Margaret's scratchy writing, which said, "Love, Margaret."

"*Dear Hanna,*

"*I hope you don't mind the typed letter. My handwriting isn't too good because of the drugs they give me, and I love to write on the typewriter. I can write more and am able to really say what I mean with the typewriter.*

"*Yes, I am in a mental hospital. But I'm okay. They just think I'm crazy. They give me a lot of pills here that make me feel tired all the time, but sometimes I have some time between the drugs when I can write. There are some really crazy people here; I don't understand why they think I'm like them.*

"*I know that we're not supposed to talk for ten years, but I think we can write. So I hope you will write back and tell me all about what you are doing. I was in school for a while, but it took up so much time away from my jump rope, so I stopped. I think that's when Mags started taking me to doctors. Anyway, at first I didn't tell them anything, not about you or Trudy or our wolves and the song and all of the stuff we did. But then they gave me all these 'treatments'—that's what they called them—and I don't remember what happened. But they said I told them things that made them put me here. So I'm not sure what they know about our wolves. I hope they don't read this.*

"*My auntie Mags comes to visit once a month. I haven't seen my mom in years; I don't know where she is, and Mags won't talk about it. So you see, I lost my mom too! And I don't have a dad either; well we don't know where he is.*

"*So Hanna, I was thinking, maybe you and Trudy can come here and tell them I'm not crazy and I can come home? I'm sorry I'm writing before it's time, but I don't want to stay here anymore, and besides, I want you to know where I am so you can find me when we're twenty. Please write back. I try every night to talk to my wolf, but they took my jump rope away and I'm not sure what to do. Maybe Trudy can tell you what I should do and you can write to me. Hanna,*

I miss you so much; I don't know what to do without you. Please help me!

"*I have one friend here who will help me get this letter to you. She's a nurse, and she told me that when she is working, I don't have to worry and she would take care of me. So when you write back, don't write to me; write to her. Her name is Neely Ash, so just put her name on the envelope.*

"*Please give Trudy a hug and a kiss from me. I love her, and I love you,*

"*Sincerely,*
"*Love Margaret*"

Trudy slowly folded the letter and set it down on the desk. Hanna sat in silence, looking at the floor. They sat in silence for a long time.

Hanna shoved her homework aside and pulled out her sketch pad and pastels, which Trudy had given her as a birthday present one year ago. She browsed through her work made every week, reflecting her feelings and hopes and dreams. She noted that her subjects had changed over the years, that her joy was constant, that the sadness she'd encountered as a young child when she lost her family had subsided, and that her love of life had not succumbed to her challenges.

She felt proud of herself, confident, and wanted to help Margaret. She wanted to express her support and love in a present for Margaret. Maybe they would let her hang it in her bedroom or wherever they made her sleep. As she took the chalk to her hand, she loved the smoothness and its smell, the color and textures she could create with it. The smoothness of the chalk made her feel smooth and free; it let her work well.

Trudy got up and began to make dinner. She wanted Hanna to be on her own for a while before they discussed the letter. She watched as Hanna self-medicated with her art and creativity and knew that she had learned well. Her ways were set, and she knew how to use her magical talents to heal herself. It was a good day. Trudy expressed her gratitude in prayer and song silently so as not to disturb Hanna.

Eventually, Hanna completed her drawing for Margaret and handed it to Trudy. "See, Trudy! Now they won't think she's making it up or that she's crazy. She can show this to her doctor, and he will see that the wolves are real, that you are real, that all that we do is real, and it is all part of our great spirit. And I know they can't tell her she's crazy if it's a religion for her, right? They aren't allowed to discriminate against her religion—I know it; we learned that in social studies. We can go there and rescue her, and she can come and live with us, right?"

"It's not that simple, Hanna. There are those who think that people who speak with spirits are witches. There are those who think we work with the devil and that we must be either insane or criminals. The path you have learned with me is not something that is considered a religion at this time. They consider it antireligion, and maybe it is. Spiritualism has existed for centuries but has always been hidden. Speaking with spirits and believing that everything is alive, including the stones, is not considered normal. I suggest that you don't go advertising what you learn with me either. No, I don't think this drawing will help Margaret. I am sorry."

"Then what can we do?"

Trudy sat down again. She looked at Hanna—into her eyes, into her soul. Hanna could feel her stare and knew that it penetrated her. She basked in the light of Trudy's gaze and the feeling it gave her inside. The heat and love filled her heart and made her cheeks red. She felt herself flush as Trudy continued to "see" her. Hanna understood that now was not the time for words. She closed her eyes, sat back in her chair, and relaxed as she had been taught. She let her spirit fly and be with her allied spirits. She felt herself splinter into bits and bask in the starlight, each piece absorbing the love of the universe, her god. And slowly, once they were recharged, they began to return—full and ready to be whole again. Like metal to magnet, they blew into place, and Hanna returned to her body. She opened her eyes after a few moments and found Trudy still staring at her and smiling brightly; Trudy's eyes shone like the stars that had filled her, and she wondered for a moment if the stars lived in Trudy's eyes.

Hanna spoke slowly. "I see only one way to help Margaret right now. All we can do is be here for her. Meaning we must keep doing what we are doing here, but all the time staying in the background for Margaret by writing to her. We will not empower her to communicate with the wolves when she is in the hospital. We will just be normal for her. So she can show she has a normal friend. I can be normal. I do it every day at school, and when I come home to you, Trudy, I know that I can be grateful for the magic and love and great spirit that we live with. So we can write to her and tell her how normal we are, and she can show it to the doctor and then maybe she can let us come and visit. I know we aren't supposed to meet until we are twenty, but this is an emergency situation, don't you think, Trudy?"

"Hanna, you must realize that you, too, are not old enough or mature enough to know what to do in this situation. I am grateful that you can receive such wisdom from the heavens in your dreamtime, but I cannot anticipate that you will know how to navigate the mental health assessment arena and how easily you could yourself get caught in it. It is like a spiderweb, you see? Things pull us to it and we open up and are judged by alien standards, and then poof! They lock you up as the spider eats her prey. No, I must make this decision with the help of someone. I think I will call Mags and maybe enlighten her on her niece's feelings. Perhaps Mags will wake up to spirit and take Margaret home. Let me work on it. Meanwhile, you mustn't let Margaret wait long for a response from you to her letter. She is fragile, and we shouldn't cause her any stress. Hanna, please write to Margaret today, and we'll get it in the mail by sunset. My sweet child, I am sad for her; give her my love."

Hanna grabbed her notebook from her book bag and tore out a couple of pages; she chose the color purple from her multicolor ballpoint pens and began to write.

"Dear Margaret,

"Thank you for your letter, which I received today. Trudy told me to write you back right away, so I hope you get this letter quickly. I am writing to the nurse like you said; I hope she isn't on vacation or something. We are confused by your situation in the hospital; you don't tell us what you have. Crazy is not the name of a disease; I looked it up. Does the doctor tell you if you are sick or what? Anyway, I want you to know that we are here and we are praying for you. In church, we will sing for you. Do you dance with the jump rope? I hope that makes you feel good. We don't know what else we can do

right now, but I think that Trudy is going to call your auntie and maybe see what happens with that. What kind of food do you eat, and what do you get to wear? Maybe we can send you some of Trudy's scones; I know you love them. Trudy says that this is not the time to play with our dogs. Okay? I love you and miss you too, and I will see you when we can.

"Hoowwwwlllll!!"
"Hanna xxxxxxxxxxx"

Hanna signed the letter and looked for an envelope.
"Are you going to share your letter with me, Hanna?" Trudy asked.
"Um, well, I don't know. Maybe not?"
"What did you write that you don't want me to see?"
"I told her we pray for her in church."
"What else?"
Hanna blurted, "Well, I just told her that you said that we shouldn't play with dogs right now. I think she'll get that, Trudy, and I don't think anyone will wonder about it if they read it. Please? I have to say something!"
"May I please see the letter? If I speak to Mags, I need to know what you wrote, Hanna. This isn't a game; you must realize that you are also under scrutiny the moment they find out about you."
"Wow, Trudy, you seem very afraid. It's not like you."
"You could be at risk, darling, and I am your protector. Remember that always. One day when you are older, you will understand; in the meantime, you still need to obey me as your guardian."
"Okay, here, it's short. I didn't write much." Hanna handed the letter to Trudy. She'd already folded it perfectly.
Trudy opened it cautiously, like she was unfolding a hot towel. As she read it, her face creased up, and Hanna wasn't sure what to think. It took a long time for her to read the one paragraph. Hanna watched every movement of her eyes and tried to figure out which part she was reading. She thought, *she's got to let me send it; I can't write another one.* The whole affair was beginning to make her feel sick. "It's crazy!" she cried. "I feel crazy all of a sudden, and it makes me sick!"

"Well, maybe we won't respond so quickly then. Your letter is okay, but it doesn't sound like it's coming from a seventeen-year-old. I've seen better writing from you. Why don't you write her a poem or something? Something very conventional."

"What's 'conventional'?"

"It means 'as usual' or something 'normal,' you might say… what I'm trying to say is no spirits and no dreams and no visions. Understood?"

"Okay." Hanna pulled some more sheets out of her notebook and stared at the blank page. She stared so hard the white of the paper with its blue lines began to rise from the page and become animated. Amused, she smiled to herself and set her pen to the paper, this time in green. She wrote:

"Dear Margaret,

"Oh softly we touch,
"Oh softly we feel,
"Oh softly we know,
"In our hearts, in our souls,
"The essence of love from mother earth,
"The shining light of father sky.
"The clouds above
"Become pillows for you
"From us.
"Be comfy, my sister.
"Be at ease, my love.
"We await you
"With open hearts and souls.
"Our hearts are with yours,
"and yours is with us.
"Oh beautiful spirit that is you,
"Margaret.
"Let you find the path to forgiveness.
"Let you arrive on the wings of joy.
"We miss your soft dream and sweet voice.
"We miss your love and your light.

*"Gratitude abounds from our connection.
"Always sister,
"Forevermore twin,
"You are to me.*

*"With love,
"Hanna"*

"How's this?" Hanna asked, giving the page to Trudy. Trudy held the page in her hands and closed her eyes without reading the words. Hanna could feel her ascending from herself. She, too, closed her eyes, and they both saw Nano and Nala looking at the page and surrounding their spiraling colors around it. It seemed to lift up out of Trudy's hand and float about in midair.

Hanna's heart filled as she knew that the wolves were adding their message to Margaret. She sat and watched as the two wolves blew light and love into the page.

Trudy smiled in her meditative state; she was relieved to see that the two wolves were together again. Nala had wandered, and Nano had let her. They knew she needed time in a solitary way, and now she had returned. Only Margaret knew what she'd gone through, and the poor soul had endured it with her. Nala's light was dim, as if tired. Her coat did not shine like Nano's, and Hanna did not feel her as much as she only saw her in her mind's eye.

Time seemed suspended as Trudy and Hanna witnessed the two working with her page and poem, working the power and charging it with a healing light that would reach Margaret. They had no access to Margaret because of the drugs she was taking. Hanna had presented them with a gift and a way to reach the child.

"Hanna, you have served your twin well. We have added medicines to your words and the physical paper. Now it is ready for you to give it to Margaret. You will go there, to the place they keep her. Trudy will take you. You will deliver the letter, but you will not see her." Nala had perked up and stood opposite Hanna, staring her in the eye as Hanna understood her words.

Trudy interjected, "Hmmmm, oh Nala, why don't you just deliver it? It's quite a distance from here, and it could cause troubles for her. We could give it to Mags to deliver. I don't know about making a trip all the way out there."

"No, this is good. You and Hanna should travel there. You will meet someone, and there is another reason you and Hanna should go." Nala moved over to her mate and shoved her nose in his belly, giving him a push. "You tell them."

"What now, Nano?" Hanna stood in front of her wolf. "What do you have in store for me now?"

Nano bowed his head and dug in the ground with his paw. He was slightly tense, and she felt it.

"Whaaaat?" Hanna tugged at his fur. He growled and walked away. Hanna followed, but she felt Trudy grab her wrist.

"Wait, Hanna. Stay here." Trudy followed the wolf, and Hanna watched intently.

Nala gave her a nudge in the back and pet her, releasing her own tension.

"What is it?" Hanna asked her.

"You will see, Hanna. Life is never simple; there's always something to trip you up. Just when you think you are okay, life falls apart."

Nala, what are you saying? Come on, I've had enough surprises. Tell me!"

Trudy returned, took Hanna in her arms, and rested her cheek on her head.

Hanna resisted and tore herself away.

Trudy told her to open her eyes and come back into the room. She said her farewells to Nano and Nala and pulled Hanna back into the room. She went and put her kettle on for tea and then gathered a few things from her shelves and brought them to the table. She laid a beautiful tapestry on the surface and began to put stones and crystals in particular spots on the cloth.

Hanna sat down in her seat at the table and watched silently.

Trudy finally spoke. "I am creating an altar for you, Hanna. It will be a place for you to pay attention over the next few days before we go and deliver the letter."

"What's it for?"

"It will be a place where you can ask the powers from all the directions and energies I have been teaching you about, kind of like a garden for them to live so that you can live with them. I want you to have a place to always feel loved. Where you can love yourself, no matter what."

"Trudy, I don't understand. What's going on? Why do I need protection?"

"That's interesting, Hanna. It is good that you see it as protection. Yes. This is good.

"Sit, my child. Sit and feel the energies of your body, your heart, and your mind. Make yourself at home with all of them. There; that is good. I see you are working well with the altar."

Trudy watched as Hanna's spirit opened to the energies she had conjured into the altar. She could see all of the anxiety drifting away and enjoyed how Hanna received the energies so well. She was ready.

"Hanna, your dad is at the same hospital as Margaret."

Hanna's body jolted to the beat of her words. She was beating her head on the table by the end of her sentence. Trudy placed her hand on her forehead to buffer the blows. Tears were streaming from Hanna's eyes as she silently rocked. Trudy wrapped her arms around her, bent slightly, and leaned in close so her heart touched her and Hanna could feel her heart beat. It was soothing to her, and Hanna began to feel less empty. Her heaving stomach subsided some, and she reached out and hugged Trudy back.

"Do I have to, Trudy? Can't I just wait till I'm older? Can't I just wait and maybe not see him till I can see Margaret again? I know, the wolves said, but I'm not ready yet."

"Well, we can put the letter in the mail, and maybe Margaret will receive it. Or we can hand deliver it, and there's more chance they will give it to her. We don't have to see your dad. He's not going to be standing there waiting for you."

"I don't know. It seems very spooky, going there. I really don't want to, Trudy. I can feel that it won't be good. Let's tell the wolves that my intuition tells me not to go!"

Trudy laughed. "Oh, Hanna, you are funny! You are really growing up."

Part II

Chapter 6

"Announcing the arrival of British Airways Flight 1232 from New York."

Hanna heard the PA system announcing Margaret's flight. Her heart flip-flopped together with her stomach. She held onto the wall for a moment to balance herself; her excitement was exploding from within, and she was having a hard time not breaking into a high-speed sprint toward the arrival gate, past security, *Oh sod 'em*, and straight onto the plane to greet her long-lost twin. She walked quickly, knowing there was nothing to hurry for—it would take ages until Margaret got through passport control and customs. In this country, England, everyone queues up for everything! Her thoughts were filled with anticipation; she knew she'd burst the moment they laid eyes on each other.

They still had a long drive ahead of them from Heathrow in England. Hanna had found herself a quiet cottage in Wales for the summer break from her university in London. This was where she and Margaret would reunite, in a valley under the Black Mountains on the River Wye.

The plane's arrival was announced again, and Hanna made her way to the arrival point, which was bordered with police barricades and a crowd of people standing in back of them, waiting too. Hanna squeezed through the crowd to get a better view and stood watching the people coming out through a shaded glass wall, with automatic sliding glass doors that opened and closed with each group of travelers passing through. The door beeped each time and alerted Hanna to look for Margaret. She watched the reunions between husbands and wives, mothers and daughters, more family, family, and more family. She knew she had none, and it hurt to watch. She knew that Margaret was now her sister, her twin, and waited to have that very same reunion—the big hug, the joy! The surprise they would have as they looked at each other for the first time in ten years! Hanna kept watching.

Then she saw her. She caught her walking, unaware still, looking out at the crowd with interest, yet calm. She had a very nonchalant movement to her. She was so cool! Hanna jumped out of her skin and let out a howl. The entire airport stared, and she didn't care. Beelining it to Margaret, she ignored the stares and the gasps and was soon in her arms as they danced in circles in the middle of the concourse. Travelers and their carts averted them, nearly crashing, and they were oblivious.

Margaret could feel Hanna's breath. Her heart warmed as she felt the hug, the jump, her voice, her howl. Not even catching sight of her yet, her bright red hair scrunched in her face, Margaret melted into her, and her eyes let the tears of a million years fall. Her body heaved up and down, and Hanna clutched her tighter as she released her missing, her mourning, and her yearning, ten years of it.

Soon enough, two towering bobbies ushered them off the concourse and into the main terminal. Hanna and Margaret unraveled their arms from each other and finally had a chance to look at each other's faces, each one beaming and exhilarating, open and anticipating. They had no words still. Another hug and another dance, until soon they plopped down on a bench.

"Margaret, I'm still so excited; I'm not ready to drive yet. Let's sit down for a cuppa tea."

"Oh Hanna, anything, I don't care, as long as I can just sit and look at you. Drive? Did you say drive? You have a car? What are you doing here anyway? Your message with the plane ticket was so short. You just said we're twenty! Drop everything and come to Wales! I didn't even know where Wales was; I had to look it up. How did you find me?"

"Let's find some tea first, Mar. Can I call you Mar? Margaret, it's so long..."

"Sure, Hanny, does that work for you?"

"Yeah, fine. Where will I find a café in this place?"

Hanna asked at information and they didn't have any, only a Wimpy's, so they walked over, hoping the tea was good.

Once they had settled, they simply sat in silence with big grins on their faces, staring into each other's eyes. They were so familiar, and both of

A Wolf Song

them suddenly felt like they had come home. There, sitting at a Wimpy's in the middle of Heathrow Airport, they were home. They felt more at ease with themselves than ever before, each of them wanting to hold onto this feeling forever. Hearing each other's thoughts, they both burst into tears and reassured each other that they would never come apart again.

Tea arrived, and they sipped on the warm drink, giggling, nearly choking on the dry biscuit provided.

"That's what you call a digestive biscuit, Mar. You choke on it; don't even get the chance to digest it! Get it?" She laughed.

"Yeah, don't they have Oreos here?" Margaret asked, pouting. They both laughed as she realized she wasn't in America. "So, Hanna, you have to explain something now. Where's all the money coming from? I've been really poor all my life, so I don't understand where all this stuff is coming from—the car, my airfare, you living in England. Where is it all coming from? Is Trudy growing money on trees or something?"

"Mar, you are better? How'd you get out of the hospital? Did you ever get our letter? Do you know my dad was at that place too?"

They realized that they both had urgent questions and laughed again.

"Do you know, I wish we could jump rope right now, here!" Mar suddenly blurted out.

"Oh, we'll have lots of time for that at my cottage in Wales, Mar. It's just paradise, right next to the river, and we won't have to jump rope any more. The wolves just come! Honest!"

Margaret was staring into space with her cup in her hands close to her lips. She closed her eyes and took a long sip of tea. "Oh, that feels good. I'm not sure if I'm hungry or not. Maybe we should go? How far is Wales from here? I guess I'm probably getting tired."

"You can sleep in the car, Mar, but you'll miss the view—it's a beautiful ride. I'll wake you when we get to the mountains."

The young women paid for their tea. Hanna grabbed some snacks and a couple of cartons of apple juice for the road, and then they made their way to Hanna's car and the "M5" westbound for Wales.

Buckled into the front passenger seat, on the wrong side of the car, looking at Hanna, her playmate from childhood in the driver's seat, was simply surreal. Margaret looked out the window. The scenery was so alien, the cars looked strange, and even the traffic lights looked different. She had imagined what Wales would look like.

"It's kind of like the mountains in the States." Hanna had read her thoughts.

Mar sat up and asked, "How'd you do that?"

"I dunno, it happens to me all the time lately. Sorry, didn't mean to intrude. My teacher said I had to watch it with my new telepathy."

"Yeah? What are you studying in London?"

"Theology, anthropology with emphasis on indigenous practices. Oh, and medieval literature as well. That's why England is the best place to study. But when I finish, I want to go and live with an indigenous tribe; I'm not sure where yet."

"Wow, wish I could. Me and Mags don't have any money; I missed most of high school in the hospital, so I never got my scores or my exams. I'd have to start again and do a GED to go to school. You were lucky, Hanna, very lucky."

"I know, Mar, so I want to share with you now. You asked before where all the money was coming from. Well, my family had a lot of money, and I got it all. We sold the house, too, and got money from that. So I can help you if you want. I can help Mags too."

"Oh, I dunno. Mags is so proud; me too. I mean, I took the ticket because I wanted to see you and the wolves again. I need my Nala, Hanna. I really do."

"Yes, and she needs you too. It's important that you find your bridges to each other again. Very important. Trudy told me to make sure you two leave together. But I hope you'll never leave; I hope you just stay here with me. We can go to school together."

"Hmm, I dunno, Hanna. Let's see. I need some sleep."

"Yeah, I guess you do. Why don't you grab the pillow from the backseat? There's a blanket back there too. Sleep for a while. You'll wake up when we get to the mountains anyway because the road's so bumpy and curvy."

Margaret slept straight through the mountain curves and didn't wake up until they arrived at Hanna's cottage. The dogs welcomed them with jumps and kisses, nearly knocking them both over.

It was dark, and Hanna ran ahead to turn on the front light and open the door.

Margaret began to unload her luggage before the dogs did; she laughed as one grabbed the handle and started pulling! "What kind of dogs are these? They are beautiful. The black sleek coat, so shiny!"

"That's 'cause they had a bath in your honor, Mar. Usually they are a danky brown-black from dust and grass stains! Love them, these two! They just love the countryside; we don't have much space in London."

"Tell me all about London, Hanna. Wow, how do you like it?"

"It's the best. It has everything. And it's not a small town. Nobody knows your business. I like that. Not like where we're from, where everybody talks about each other. Here they are English, and they don't pry. I like that. 'Specially since I don't always share the stuff I learned with Trudy, and it's hard to explain at school sometimes that I've actually practiced some of the things we are learning about in theory. I just keep it to myself."

They were still standing in the foyer, and the dogs were still jumping and waiting for their dinner. Hanna dropped everything to feed them in the kitchen. "Your room is upstairs, first room on your right. I hope you like the view; oh, but you won't see anything now that it's dark. Go on up, Mar; make yourself at home. I'll just feed the dogs and get us some dinner together. We should have stopped at the Chinese takeaway when we drove through town. Never mind; I'll make us some cheese on toast."

"What's that?" Hanna heard Margaret say as she climbed the stairs.

"Oh, it's just like grilled cheese, but I put tomatoes on it too. How does that sound? And I have pie for dessert."

"Pie sounds good."

Hanna laughed and continued in the kitchen with the dogs and their dinner.

Margaret opened the first door on the right with her eyes closed, bursting with anticipation. Her room. First time ever. She switched on the light and took in a deep breath and opened her eyes. It smelled of lavender and pine. The whole house smelled of a wood fire. The room was small and cozy. Freshly painted, she could tell, with a plush salmon-color carpet. A single bed was in the corner and a desk near the rooftop window. Margaret pulled in her bags and kicked off her boots. She sat down on the bed, which bent with her, and she patted the pillow and held it to her cheek. It smelled of lavender that nearly sent her to sleep.

She resisted the temptation and began to unpeel her clothes, starting with her jacket; the more layers she removed, the more she wanted a bath. She wandered out onto the landing half dressed, looking for the bathroom.

"Last door on your right," she heard Hanna call up and smiled to herself.

"Thanks, twin," Mar called back. "I'm going to have a bath, Hanna; it should revive me for an hour, so enough time for dinner."

There were soft thick towels hanging on warm pipes in the bathroom. Margaret had never seen anything like it. The bathtub was like something out of a museum. It was white and it stood upright on its own feet and was deep as a hot tub! She turned on the water and sprinkled in some bath salts she found on the shelf. The room was so cute, with white curtains and the most beautiful lace shower curtain; she pulled it out of the tub and tied it away from the water. Soon the bath was full, and Margaret sank deep under the bubbles and let herself submerge. She lay there for as long as she could hold her breath and then sat up and soaked until Hanna came up with the sandwiches.

Hanna perched herself on the side of the tub, and they ate their dinner.

"Oh Mar, I have so many plans for us; it's going to be the best summer. Tomorrow we'll just hang out at the river; you'll probably be napping a lot because of the jet lag, so there's no sense going anywhere. Does that work for you, Mar?"

Mar was already sleeping. Hanna woke her up and helped get her dried off and to bed.

Margaret woke with the sunrise. She was wide-awake, and she stood in front of the window in the corner. It faced east, and her view was spectacular. Margaret stepped back for a moment; she had never seen such natural unlandscaped beauty where she was from. They were in a valley, with mountains towering to either side. The valley was an emerald green, a shade she'd only seen in movies. The farmland was all divided by dark green hedges, which grew wildly; she noticed some cropped and some not.

A Wolf Song

Each homestead bore houses and barns, and this morning as the pink and golden sunrise glowed on the greens and browns, Margaret could feel and taste and smell the wonder of it.

She grabbed her robe and ran downstairs and out the door. She didn't realize how chilly it was, and she braced herself once the cold set in. The morning air was brisk and fragrant. She breathed deeply, with her face up to the sky toward the sun in the east, and let her arms spread out like a bird. She had never felt another place before, not really. The air here was different; everything was different!

Margaret danced about the front yard, knowing she could and no one would mind. Knowing somehow that now she was safe and they wouldn't be sending her to another hospital. She felt a song come to her and remembered Hanna's song that she'd received in the hospital.

"Ahhhhhh, I'm finally on my own!"

The dogs heard her and came down to the front door, scratching at it and barking. Margaret let them out, and they leaped all over her, slobbering her with their long tongues and floppy ears, their fur—deep black and silky—waving in long droves down their legs and back. Margaret followed as they took to the back of the house, where she found a stone patio and table with chairs, a rocking swing and a rose garden on the side.

It reminded her of Trudy's garden, and her stomach tightened as she remembered their beginnings. She thought, *Hanna seems to have done well and recovered from losing her family, and oh, the violence!* Margaret still didn't understand how Hanna had recovered so well. It was something she must remember to ask her.

Later in the morning, after breakfast, Margaret and Hanna packed up a picnic lunch and set out to the river. The dogs followed and led all the way; they loved days at the river, too, and were in a hurry to get there.

The river was full and moving swiftly westward. They stopped to settle under some alder trees where the river took a turn; there were huge boulders in the middle that they could wade over to. The other side of the bend curved drastically, creating a small pond-like inlet where the water was still.

They settled on a soft step where the boulders provided backrests and the ground was mosslike. Hanna spread a couple of blankets, as she knew the dogs would join them. They set down the food, and both lay down flat on the ground for a moment, looking up at the sky. The clouds were big and lumpy, their gray hues intensified and softened with the sunlight, and Hanna and Margaret giggled as they pointed out all of the formations that they could see within the clouds. "There's an eagle!" one said, and the other said, "And you see the branch he's standing on. There's another one right above him on a higher cloud!"

"Ah, Hanna, it's been so long since I could stretch my imagination again with no judgment. Thank you! I keep saying it, thank you!"

"No, thank you for coming all this way, Margaret. I knew we had to meet this summer, and I knew I couldn't come back to the States, not now, when there are places like this!"

"I've been so excited about showing you this wonderful country, Mar. I do hope you stay awhile. Well, maybe we should catch up a bit before we make future plans. I don't know what the wolves have for us, but we'll be working with them this summer, I know."

"Do you talk with them every day, Hanny?"

"Not every day when I'm at school, but a lot, and they come in sometimes when I'm studying because they want to add something. It's strange, but it's good. Trudy would do that, and now they do. Trudy would come to me while I was reading history or something, and she would act out the scene I was reading about, like she was there. And sometimes the story wasn't the same. Trudy says that you have to be picky when you read and study, be careful not to learn other people's judgments, other people's belief systems. Anyway, I've been out here a month since school broke for summer, and every day I come out here and meet the wolves and Trudy. They continue to teach me about trust. It's about finding my way in life physically and spiritually."

"Let's have some berries!"

Hanna pulled a container out of the picnic basket and another container that Margaret didn't recognize. She picked it up and asked, "What's clotted cream?"

"It's the best thing ever produced by a cow, Mar. You will love it with the berries. Here, take a dollop; you don't need much."

Margaret's eyes crossed with delight from the berries and clotted cream. Her grin let a drop of purple juice drool, and Hanna caught it with her napkin. "Isn't that good?"

"The best, Hanny. I'm going to get fat here; it must be fattening!"

"So, Margaret, tell me your story now. I want to hear everything, all of it from when your house burned down. It's time."

Margaret felt mixed about going back so long. She squirmed a bit and rolled around the blanket like a cat, stretching and yawning; then she sat back up and looked Hanna keenly in the eye. "Are you sure? It isn't pretty, Hanny. I don't know; well, let me see." She pushed herself up against the sun-warmed boulder behind and dug her shoes in the ground. "Well, it's like this, Hanna. Not much really happened. Well, you know, a lot did, but not really. I mean, we didn't move a lot or anything. Mags and my mom are still at the same house out of town in the middle of nowhere, and it still is the middle of nowhere. All I did there was stand in the backyard all the time, and that's when they started taking me to the doctors. My mom never was the same since the fire. I went to school sometimes, and I even had a kind of friend for one year. What else?"

"Wow, Mar, I'm sorry; I didn't realize how painful it would be for you. Let's try something for a moment. Here, come over here and lay your head in my lap."

Margaret moved over to Hanna and carefully rested her head. It felt so good and strange too.

"Now, Mar, I want you to close your eyes and concentrate on your breathing. Take long breaths in and out, and hold it for a moment too. Just let your mind slip away and relax into the wonderful fragrances of this place. Breathe in and out."

Soon enough Margaret could feel the brush of fur on her cheek. She knew there was no one to harm her and didn't stir from her breathing. She felt them; they were with her again, finally. She felt full.

"Mar, can you see them yet?" Hanna asked quietly.

Mar nodded and smiled with her eyes closed.

"Now listen."

Nala's familiar voice said, "Oh girl, good to have you in our presence again. I am pleased with you; you found Margaret for your twentieth anniversary. Our twentieth anniversary. We celebrate this union. All those who are with us," she howled, turning her nose to the sky, "all those who accompany us on our path of heart, be with us now in celebration! We are joyous and prevailing; our intent is true, and we see it here and now. You have come together, dear girls, and I am reunited with you." She turned to Nano and twisted round him. He let out a soft snarl at her in approval and sniffed her butt. She leaped over him and back again playfully, and Margaret smiled watching them.

"So, Mar," Hanna started quietly, "do you remember sending us that letter from King's County?"

"What letter? I received one from you; it came from a lady who worked there. I have no idea how she got it because she wasn't the mail lady and she brought it to me personally. Actually it was after I received your letter with that beautiful poem with no mention of our wolves that I realized you were real."

"What do you mean, real?" Hanna asked.

"Well, I got so crazy with all of the stuff that we learned afterward that I started to believe all of the daydreams I had with you and the wolves, and it became my complete reality for a while. That's when all the trouble started. Or rather, maybe that's when I really went crazy. You know how we used to talk about imagination and what we saw was real in another dimension? Well, I think I just totally moved into that dimension and couldn't come back. Well, not till they gave me a load of drugs and 'treatments' with electricity and also swimming; they made me swim.

"I don't know; at one point I became aware of myself again. Me, here on earth, and it was when I read your poem that I saw that you were living your life, that you were real here in the physical, and it pulled me back to me. Hanny, I was out there someplace; I didn't care about anything.

"I stopped eating to start with, so they had me in a children's hospital for a while trying to get me to eat. I did start eating there, and then I came home and Mags sent me to school. It was a horrible place, and the kids were really mean. I tried just to jump rope in the school yard most of the time, but there were bullies, and also kids used to bring their dogs to school and they were pretty scary too. I don't know, so I was in school for a while, and then I figured out that if I went outside in the morning to jump rope and just ignored Mags when she called, she would leave me alone and not make me go. Then a few weeks of that, and they took me to see another doctor.

"I went back and forth, Hanny, for a long time. I never saw my mom, even though we lived in the same house. I don't know when she would come out of her room, but I never saw her. Sometimes, if I put my ear to the door, I would hear her in her room, moving or something. I don't know what was wrong with her, and Mags wouldn't talk about it when I asked. So I stopped asking.

"In fact, I stopped talking too. That's when they sent me to Kings County. I was there for a good four years, I think. They let me go when I was eighteen, said I was free to stay or go because I was an adult. They told me that Mags kept me there until I turned eighteen. That was a shock. I didn't know she could have taken me home."

Yes, well, we found that out the hard way when Trudy called her and asked her to take Mar out and she wouldn't, Hanna thought to herself. "It was a shock to us too."

"Maybe I really was crazy, Hanny. I certainly didn't feel like I do now. Today, I feel like I'm here on earth, and I love this present moment. That feeling is very special to me. It's so *now!*"

Nala perked up. "Margaret, my spirit child, my body on earth, you have learned well. You have taken yourself to your limits, as I have. You have found your core self, and I have watched you and looked for my own. We have traveled well together. I let you know that most of your dreams were real, but not for this physical world you are in. You will learn to keep your wisdom and hold it to you. To share it only to those who ask and are open to you and your path of heart."

"Path of heart. You keep saying that," Mar said.

Nala replied, "Yes, you are on a path of heart; you just don't know it yet, child."

"Does it mean that I live honestly? Does it mean truth? I need truth; I need to touch things and not just trust right now, as I don't trust my sanity. It's very thin, that line we have between our sane selves and our insane selves. Wolf, how do I know?"

"That is part of the unknowable," Nano interrupted. He stood tall between them, and Hanna paid attention too. "Life is a mixture of sane and insane. Unconditional love and trust seem impossible in the world. If you are diligent and use your intuition, you will know what serves you and what does not. This opens the gateway to trust, as you trust yourself in your diligence as well."

"Well, you guys just tell me if I'm crazy, because I've stopped all of the drugs and who knows what could happen!" Margaret laughed.

"Mar, when did you do that?" Hanna asked.

"It's been about a year now, and things have been okay. I got a job at the local supermarket and started contributing to the house, and that was good for Mags. I think I'm living in the now, now. I don't know how to describe the feeling it is—kind of like a wolf without us as his or her physical self. Yeah, how would you feel if we disappeared on you? Wouldn't you start to imagine us as real?"

That struck a hard chord with her wolf. Margaret didn't realize that Nala had journeyed these years with her and that her insanity was the wolf's and that the wolf's was hers. She didn't realize how interlinked they really were.

She said, "Margaret, I've said this before: what you experience, I experience, just in a different way. Do you see what our task was? Learning the difference between me and you. In order to learn it, you had to experience it to the extreme. So did I. I have spent the last millennium in solitude. I have learned to take the lonely road so that I may be my own ally, so that I may fulfill what is needed in my path. To fulfill myself and share with you on earth. I am ready, my twin, my body; I am ready to walk in unison with you."

Margaret cried as she remembered Nala's essence and felt her resonating all over. She felt complete and full. She was ready to open her eyes and be with the river and with Hanna.

As they came out of their dream, they opened their eyes to find both dogs asleep on the blanket. One had brought a large branch with him, and it too was on the blanket. Hanna loosened it from his grip, and he stirred for a moment as he tracked where she put the stick. She opened the picnic basket in search of something good to munch on and a drink. "Mar, want something?"

"Yeah, any of that apple juice?"

"Yeah, here," Hanna said and gave Margaret the juice. "We have scones and jam and cream; shall I make you a plate?"

"Oh yes, please. That clotted cream is delicious—never had anything like it!"

The two sat with their scones and cream, and the dogs sniffed away and begged for crumbs; the river flowed past, giving them a chorus of bubbles and splashes. Soon enough, the two were fed and playing among the rocks in the water, barefooted and jeans rolled up to their knees.

"These rocks are so slippery," Hanna commented, while Mar climbed up a warm gray granite boulder and lay there on its surface, soaking up the sunlight from both sides. Hanna saw Mar all content and splashed water up the rock. Margaret turned away, only to fall over the other side straight into the water.

Soaked and dripping, Margaret waded out to their beach. They hadn't brought towels, and a wind had picked up. She stood quite freezing as Hanna joked and splashed more water on her. "Stop it, Hanna, enough! I'm freezing!"

"Well, teach ya, Mar. You have to be careful in the river!"

"You shoulda warned me," Mar protested and got up and stomped off.

"There ya go leaving, without anything?" Hanna gathered up their blanket and picnic basket and the food and trailed behind her, calling, "Mar, you want to give me a hand with all this stuff?"

Mar stopped and grabbed the blankets, quickly turning back to her stomp back to the cottage.

"Well, be like that then," Hanna complained and said no more until they reached home.

The dogs raced back and forth at their side, full of anticipation.

Hanna felt deflated and wondered if things with Margaret would always be so difficult.

When they returned, Margaret turned in for a nap.

Hanna remembered she was jet-lagged and probably cranky because of that.

"I have a prayer that I made up, that used to get me through the really bad times, Hanna. Maybe I should say it now; I feel so weak all of a sudden," Mar said as she came down the stairs after her nap. "How long did I sleep?"

"Oh, a couple of hours. Here, I'll put the kettle on and make tea."

"You sound so English!" Margaret commented and wondered suddenly who Hanna really was. "Some of you is so familiar, and some of you... I just don't know you at all."

A Wolf Song

"Margaret, I love you, and I will never try to hurt you. You just have to trust me, right? Yes, over here they drink a lot of tea, but I used to drink a lot of tea with Trudy too, so no, that's not English for me. I feel like you are trying to get at me."

"I'm not, Hanna. I'm just thinking about everything. It's all so new, and I've never seen anything like this; I didn't study England at school or anything, so this place is pretty foreign to me. And it's making me feel foreign."

"Well, Mar, why don't you just consider it your dream come true?"

Margaret stood back and retorted, "'Cause it's not my dream come true! It's yours! I mean, it is..." Her light faded and reemerged. "It was my dream for us to reunite. But all the rest? England, this cottage, your life! It's all so rich! I'm not used to it. And all you have been through, and ten years living with Trudy! I feel so out of it! And what's more, you know, I do have dreams about the future; well, I keep having this dream that our time together is short. I keep seeing that we will only see each other every ten years or so. *And it kills me, Hanna*! It hurts me so much, 'cause I know we will have to separate again."

Margaret's words came like bullets in Hanna's heart. She stared at Margaret, her mouth wide-open, her eyes questioning, and her brow all scrunched. "Huh?" she uttered. "What are you talking about? I never... nobody ever said... Trudy never... well, I guess I never asked. I just assumed this was it. I thought our separation was over."

"I don't know, Hanny. Maybe it's my fear of separation that's bringing the dream, but it's pretty clear. My Nala keeps running off in the dream, and then I go chasing her, and that always means leaving you. Me and my dreams..." she lamented.

"What's for sure is I didn't dream your dad would kill your family," Margaret said out of the blue.

Hanna perked up; she was sprawled on an antique chaise longue with paisley tapestry upholstery and sculptured feet. "No, no one could have predicted that, Mar. Hmmm, how do I say it? There's a word that the Native Americans use; Trudy taught me it when we talked about my dad. It's called Heyoka. It's everything the opposite, so whatever we expected to happen, would not, and all of the unthinkable did. The absurd, the contrary. Your dreams of what will, could or would not have seen this

Heyoka as it stays hidden in the mystery, the unknown, and pops out when least expected. It tests us; it wakes us up."

"You mean, bad things have to happen for us to wake up?" Mar asked.

"No, that's not what I mean, but we should talk about that; what I mean is that you can't foresee the unknown, and when you try to… it's like watching a dog chasing its tail. It will drive you crazy. Maybe that's what made you crazy, Mar—trying to experience or know the unknown. That would make me crazy!"

"Yes, Hanny, I did try and used my dreaming abilities, and probably too hard, because I became crazy with things I thought were real, but weren't. There's a difference between the imagination we use to talk to our wolves and what I was doing; I was not honoring what was a dream and what was here on earth. Even in your imagination, you can't make-believe the earth doesn't exist and live in the dream all of the time."

Margaret started to speak again but hesitated, wondering whether to say it or not; she didn't want to offend Hanna and wasn't sure if her question would offend her.

"What?" Hanna asked. "What do you want to ask?"

"Well, you said that your dad is at Riverpark, where I was but in a different ward. I'm just wondering what kind of crazy makes someone do what he did and how did you forgive him, because you don't seem too upset about it," she blurted out.

Hanna sat up and leaned forward toward Margaret, who was sitting in an old bentwood rocking chair; it creaked as she rocked. When Hanna came forward, she grabbed Margaret's hand and caught her eye.

"Mar," she said, "you are right; I have forgiven him. There is so much still to tell you. We can't separate so soon, Margaret. Promise me you'll stay here at least till the end of the summer! Mar, you can't go so soon." She held Mar's hand tight as she rocked back and then forward again.

"I feel that something life-changing will be happening here in this place," Margaret said, staring into Hanna's eyes. Her voice was low and soft and had a little bit of an accent. Hanna had never heard her like this. Suddenly Margaret stood and looked into the fire in the fireplace. Her voice sounded to Hanna like it was coming from somewhere else.

"I am that wrinkle in your shirt.

"I am the one who bothers you.

"You are my heart's home,
"and yours is home with me.
"You guide; I follow.
"I fall; you know how.
"Twin, you, that you be me and I be you.
"We move and jump
"or skip another hoop."

Hanna said, "You didn't answer my question, Mar. Will you stay for the summer, at least?"

"Yes, Hanna, I will, but I don't think we are going to be alone. I know someone is coming. Could it be Trudy?"

"What a great idea, Mar. I will call her and see if she wants to come over! It's morning her time, so we should catch her."

"No, Hanna, I don't think we have to."

"What do you mean?" Hanna asked, confused.

"I think she's here, Hanna. I feel her, just for the last few minutes. I keep feeling her inside me."

Just then, the dogs' ears perked up simultaneously, and they rose toward the door, circling each other. Hanna and Margaret watched and then heard a small commotion outside; they joined the dogs, who were now barking, next to the door.

Hanna pulled the curtain and looked out of the window next to the door. It seemed she was looking at dust settling. She saw swirls landing on the ground like tiny tornadoes, and in the center, there was an image that very slowly materialized. The four of them stood in awe as they watched Trudy materialize in the front yard.

Chapter 7

Not only was Trudy materializing in the front yard; the dogs suddenly began barking as if another dog had entered their territory. The front door, now ajar, revealed the entire picture. There they were: Nano, Nala, and Trudy quietly orienting themselves in the front of Hanna's cottage.

Hanna and Margaret ran outside and closed the dogs indoors. They hugged Trudy and their wolves, and there was a wonderful air of silence but celebratory joy within them all as they quietly communed and laughed and circled each other in a reunion dance.

"Wow, that was some grand entrance, Trudy! How did you manage that?" Margaret asked once Trudy was settled on the wooden bentwood rocking chair. Her hair was still standing on end and she hadn't removed her coat, saying it was cold.

Hanna stoked the fire and threw on a few extra logs, bringing the flames to a steady burn; she prayed the wind wouldn't turn and send smoke billowing down the chimney into the house.

Hanna brought Trudy an extra blanket and put the kettle on for hot tea. Trudy's luggage was full of herbs she had brought over from her garden. They even found a couple of drums and rattles in one bag.

Margaret checked out each item with wonder. Hanna resisted sharing every detail she knew about these items from Trudy's house; she knew Trudy would do that herself. The wolves had settled in front of the fire; they seemed content, and Hanna had put the dogs upstairs in her bedroom.

The kettle boiled, and Hanna and Margaret served up tea and crumpets to Trudy. There was some fruit salad in the fridge, which Hanna also put on the table with some hard cheddar and a cutting board. Hanna was very proud of her new English food skills. The first few months she was here, she fed out of McDonalds because the food was so alien and she just didn't know what to do with it or what to order at restaurants.

"Trudy, you didn't answer my question. How did you get here, and how is it we can see the wolves? Did they bring you?" Margaret asked demandingly.

Trudy pulled a broom out from her side and said, "I don't know about the wolves. I'm not even sure they are your wolves." She nudged one and smiled, asking, "Who are you?" Nano growled playfully and licked Trudy's ankle.

Trudy handed the broom to Margaret. "You know, Margaret, for a medicine woman like me to journey to this enchanted land of Wyrrd, there would only be two ways." She looked over at Margaret and added, "Either on the wing of a phoenix or on a broomstick of alder wood and lavender stalks. This isn't a good time for the phoenix to be making intercontinental flights, so I just got on my broomstick! Who are those wolves?" She laughed and cajoled Margaret.

Hanna was smiling and laughing with her. "How do you think Trudy got here, Mar?" Hanna asked.

"Well, I remember when her house appeared out of nowhere when we first met her, so it didn't really surprise me that she just 'appeared' in the front yard." Margaret continued, "I don't know, it's probably something magical, and I know you can't explain magic, so don't bother trying. If you just 'appeared' here, then okay. I am just so happy to see you all, I don't care anymore how you got here!"

"Margaret, there is a big lesson in your words. I hope you see it," Trudy said.

"I do, Trudy, thank you. There are some things that I completely know, and you don't have to teach me anything; and there are other things that I don't even know exist. Like just before we were saying that you should come here. Hanna was about to phone you when you arrived in the front yard. Did you know that?"

Trudy laughed. "No, Margaret, I can't hear anything from here when I'm traveling!" She laughed and slapped her thigh.

Margaret frowned, feeling mocked, and turned away to sit with the wolves. She lay down and rested her head on one of them; she didn't even look to see which one. She didn't understand why Trudy was laughing at everything. Mar was so excited and wanted to share so much with her; she thought Trudy would give her all the answers, but it seemed right now that Trudy wanted her to find the answers herself. The unknown was so unsettling for her. She had just spent ten years in a state of the unknown, and now that she was back with her pals, she wanted to *know… everything.*

"Margaret, I have brought some new things with me. It's good for you to feel friction from me and the way I talk to you. It opens you up to learn; it moves you. We will learn much this summer. Hanna, have you been down to the river with Margaret yet?"

"Yes, Trudy, we were there today, but how do you know about the river? You've never been here."

"Don't you suppose for one moment, Hanna, that maybe I have been here in past times? Maybe I know this place better than you? Maybe I sent you here?"

"Wow, and I thought I found this magical place all by myself! I've been watching all of the things that happen here… like with the dogs. We've got two wolves sitting in their home, and they seem to be fine; they're quiet upstairs, eh?" Hanna went into the kitchen although still within earshot.

"Hanna, we are in a very magical place," Trudy said as her voice changed. She closed her eyes, and words came from her mouth, though she seemed to be another… "It is a power center for the world of Wyrrd. Some call it the underworld, the place of fairies, elves, and trolls, a world where magic is ordinary and the church is not trusted. They live in the shadow world but emanate light to the universe. This summer we will experience existence from difference directions, my dears. We will be seeing the past and the present. We will be witnessing another present. You will see. Yes, yes indeed, my daughters, we will be looking at things from another perspective. From within these experiences, you will begin to witness real power."

"Power?" Margaret perched up on one elbow from her bed of fur. She rubbed her nose and continued, "What do you mean by power?"

"Power is the joy in what you do and are. Power is the fuel that takes you where you want to go. Power stalks you and mirrors itself in heroes; it sends out bread crumbs to you in others' deeds. You can be inspired by power, you can be energized, but it will only aid you if you take it. Power won't come to you and beg; it will only entice you."

Hanna came in from the kitchen, where she'd been starting dinner and tidying up a bit. "Power? You all talking about power? You know, Trudy, I still don't get that one exactly. Like, I know I am very fortunate and can basically do what I please because I have the funds. But I also know that if I didn't have confidence and self-love, I would never have left your home and started a new life in England and Wales. I could have had all the money in the world, but without the power to get up and do it, I would have stayed paralyzed with you. Is that what you mean by power?"

Margaret wondered if she, too, had come onboard with power.

Trudy answered for her. "Margaret, you performed a great 'act of power' by taking the ticket Hanna offered you and coming to a strange country to see her, ten years later. Yes, that is power. You both have made enormous acts of power, and I am so very pleased with your progress. Margaret, you will have to sit down with me and tell me about the experiences you have had and where you want to go. We have much to discuss. Hanna, I have brought a book for you. I believe you are ready to read this teacher's books. She writes many, and she brings the ancient knowledge of woman forward to us in a beautiful fictional-type way. She is a friend and a sister in circle, and it is time that I introduced you to her books."

"What about me?" Margaret asked. "Can't I read the book too?"

Trudy reached out to Margaret and wrapped her hand around her neck. Margaret turned and reached back and looked at Trudy pleading, her eyebrows drawn up and mouth open; Trudy stuffed a piece of crumpet in her mouth and patted her head.

"Margaret, you too can read the book. Of course. Sorry, we will get reacquainted, my dear. You have been through so much, and I want to work with you some before you read this book, *Medicine Woman*. It is a great book about power, feminine power, the way we work, the way we are the recipients, just like mother earth..." Trudy's eyes glazed over as she spoke; you could feel her spirit leaving for another plane.

The girls laughed and poked Trudy, and she came back with a smile from a distant past. "Yes, just speaking of this book takes me to another place and time, ladies. Oh my dear ladies, how you've both grown up so! Let me look at you!"

The celebrations among them carried on late in the night, and when they all finally turned in, the chorus of howls, barks, and angelic harmony faded and silenced the house. Trudy lay in her bed, which Hanna had set up for her in the studio downstairs off of the kitchen; she and the wolves settled there. The dogs came down back down stairs and lay in front of the fire place, in awe of the wolves, who were within their scent range. They sniffed and licked each other as they humbly pawed their noses.

Trudy could see out of the spot window in the middle of the arched ceiling above her. Her room was a converted shed, once stone-walled, with a roof made of faggots of bramble and sticks, now replaced with shingles and sun windows. Trudy knew this house from years gone by; the cow lived in her room, and she would come out here in the morning for the milking and feeding. She felt herself drift back to that time; it was another life that she remembered well.

Maybe three to four hundred years back, in a time when this land was settled by the magical people who worshipped the earth and who hid in the forests and the caves from the clergy and members of the church. It was a time like today, when real power was feared by the power holders. Self-empowerment and ownership threatened the powers that be, and it caused the magical people to go underground.

Trudy was walking through a village that she knew well. She could hear the river by her side, and the sound of the wind coming down from the black mountains, which stood behind the village and shadowed over them early each day. This daily life centered around the spare hours of sunlight; most power here was influenced by the sun or the lack of it. She felt her deep connection with this land and instinctively knew where she was going and what position the sun would be in when she got there. As she followed the stream of light filtering through the trees now, she knew that later in the day, she would be sensing it in the shadow of the mountain. This was a sense only known by the people who lived in the shadow—the ability to see and feel light when enveloped in shadow.

The next day at breakfast, Trudy was fast to impart her dreams of the night before. Once the wolves and the dogs had had their morning run and they had all gathered in the kitchen, Trudy blurted out, "Today, girls, I will teach you to feel and sense the shadow, so that it becomes a sense to you. This is the land where light came out of the shadow. In her honor, we shall experience this lesson here."

Hanna was busy at the cooker, frying up everything in sight, a typical British tradition; Trudy sniffed the fry-up, which gave her terrible heartburn, and asked Hanna to make her a hard-boiled egg and some toast. Margaret was ready to eat up anything Hanna made, and the two ate everything she cooked; they weren't paying much attention to Trudy.

When they all sat down, Trudy announced that they would be going down to the river directly after breakfast. After that, they would drive into town for food. Hanna suggested they have fish and chips for dinner in town, and with that, the day was planned.

Down on the riverbank, they'd settled down on the soft moss-covered beach. Hanna pulled some snacks from the basket: a couple of bags of cheese and onion crisps and pork scratchings—the good ones in the white and black bag. While the girls were eating, Trudy pulled numerous articles from her bag; one would wonder how they all fit in there. When she was finished, the blanket was covered end-to-end with what she called "sacred tools."

There were drums, rattles, sticks and ribbons, feathers, books, tapestries, and crystals… lots of crystals. Sprigs of herbs were scattered everywhere, and they could smell a deep scent of sage, which was burning to the side lying in a multihued abalone shell. Trudy had positioned everything in relation to how it reflected the sun's rays; the crystals formed lines in the landscape seen on the surface and also like laser beams in the sky. They created forms that the girls observed. The forms changed in the light. Margaret and Hanna followed the light, and danced the dance of reflection with each pyramid, square, and cube. Crosses interjected with circles, and lines squiggled out of the boundaries where shadows lay.

It was into the shadows that Trudy sent Hanna and Margaret after they had felt the light. As they walked from their brilliant space into the shadow, the girls felt it's weight in their hearts as they experienced the place where no light would shine. Then one spotted a crystal and brought it over. They walked with it held high to the sky, so maybe it would catch a ray, a sight of light. And eventually it did, and they had the sheer joy of shining the light into the shadow. But not before hours of trying to conceive where the light would come from and how they might be able to create it from themselves.

Then they sat down with Trudy and the wolves to talk about what had happened.

"Well, Trudy," Margaret started; she was bursting with an idea, and her whole body was shimmering with delight. "I think I know why you have brought us this lesson. Most of life is in the shadow—well, my life has been. And I can see and feel the escape route when I look for the light. It's kind of like when I was in the hospital and everything seemed dark; then one day I got that letter from Hanna, and your light seemed even brighter because I was in the shadow. I became my shadow and sometimes light hurt, but at least I could feel it and see it and I knew the light had love. I always remembered love. Anytime there was kindness, I would remember love. Shadow is a point of view, Trudy; it depends on how you look at it, right?"

Trudy smiled and reached over and hugged Margaret. "You are a smart cookie, Ms. We are going to enjoy our time together."

Hanna joined in. "I understand this too. But I think it's more important that we learn how to recognize the shadow. You know me, Trudy; I'm so trusting, I never really see when I have entered a dark place."

She walked over to Nano, who was sitting to the side of their circle. He raised his head up to her. She caressed him and scratched his ears. "Wolf, you were so very good about taking care of me and teaching me when all that killing happened, that I am still a very trusting person. I never really feel where the danger is, and I guess I've just been very lucky, because my life has been danger-free since all that happened."

Nano licked her hand and howled up to the sky. "Yes, you are free of the hardness most people have. Even Margaret—she has been hardened. Her mom left her but stayed in the physical. She created a shadow in the home. But Margaret didn't have the tools to find light in the shadows, so she did what she did know."

"Yeah," Margaret interrupted, "I went outside and jumped rope. Sometimes I found you, Nala, but most times I didn't. It was heartbreaking when I couldn't find you, because then I would create my own shadow of self-doubt; those were the days when I would just jump for hours at a time."

Hanna asked, "Mar, what would pull you out of it when you just kept jumping? I mean, didn't you get hungry or go to the bathroom? I suppose what I'm asking is, were you aware of yourself in the shadow? That's what I can't do; I never know until I leave that place that I was there… know what I mean?"

Trudy got up and picked up her rattle and began to shake it around both of the girls. She had a feather in her other hand, and as she rattled, she gently patted the air around them.

"With this vibration that I bring to you,
"through the sound of the pearls that dance inside
"the cows hide and gives you a heartbeat
"rhythm to follow.
"Let the love and light always be within you.
"It will be your mirror and your shield.
"It will serve you and guide you
"When shadows glow."

"I have seen many dark things," Margaret said and drifted, her eyes shifting to the ground and her presence fading. Nala got up and circled her. Margaret was weeping quietly, her wolf standing with her in her shadow.

Trudy continued to rattle around them. She chanted in an unrecognizable language, and Hanna simply closed her eyes and tried to join in with the chant.

"Wolf, you don't know what I've been through," Margaret cried. "I nearly couldn't come back a few times, and I still feel that; it sits and stalks me sometimes."

"Not come back to where, Mar?" Nala asked.

"There were times when I didn't know who anyone was, when all I could see myself as was a big hole that somehow I had to feed."

"You were looking into your own source, Mar, because it was bereft of the love and guidance that you searched for, a vacuum created within you. It takes many strengths to climb from a self-made void. First you need intent, which means you need a very good reason. Then you need to know that you are good enough to have what you want. Your survival, little one, tells us that you are ready to learn the old way. We will not be separate again."

Margaret hugged Nala and began to feel a fullness in her belly. It felt like a ball of love, and it spread all over her body. It was warm, it was comfy—no rocks or glass to look out for; she lay down on what felt like a bed of feathers and fell into a deep sleep.

"We will leave Margaret here with her wolf, Hanna. Come; let us walk," Trudy said and put her hand up toward Hanna for hers. Hanna pulled her up, and they wandered down to the bank of the river and started walking downstream at water's edge. Nano followed closely behind, leaving Margaret alone with Nala.

Hanna's dogs had gotten out of the house and had joined them early on. They seemed to have accepted the wolves and were not paying much attention to them.

When Hanna walked off, they followed but stayed behind Nano. Hanna wasn't sure how much the dogs could see the wolves, but she knew they certainly sensed them. She wondered if spirits had scents and made a mental note to ask.

"So, dear one, shall we sit here for a spell?" Trudy had found a little enclave of rocks that created a small pool where the water was quiet and warm. "I might just take a dip in the pool! Want to join me?"

"Trudy, it's kinda chilly; I don't want to get wet," Hanna responded, but Trudy took no notice and pushed her gently, and she tipped over straight into the water!

Nano dived in straight after her, and Trudy followed. Underwater, Hanna could not feel the difference between being above water and below. Her breathing remained the same, and she could see and hear just like on land. She even felt dry. She noticed that the pool was much larger than how she'd perceived it from the bank. She could see for miles around her, and the floor was a sea of darkness. Her swimming was impeccable; even though she couldn't swim on earth, she saw far ahead a structure of some kind and she swam to it.

When she arrived, she realized that they were joining a large gathering; as Hanna, Trudy, and Nano entered this realm, they were no longer in the water but on dry land. The structure she had seen was an ancient ruin she knew. It was Stonehenge, a pagan ancient site she had visited and studied in school. She knew this place was sacred, but Trudy had never mentioned it and she was quite surprised that Trudy had guided her to this place. "Trudy, this place! I've been here! We have been studying it at Uni!"

Trudy hushed her, as they were entering some kind of ceremony. They stood in the outskirts of the circle but could see the fire in the center and a few people who seemed to be in animal costumes; they wore masks and were dancing and chanting and playing drums, flutes, and rattles.

Hanna's attention rested on the rattles. Most everyone had one but her. She asked Trudy, who gave her one from the deep pockets of her apron. It was of a medium size, and its sound was almost metallic. As Hanna shook it quietly to her ear, she could see the waves of the ocean rushing in. She smiled as Trudy caught her eye, and they gazed at each other and listened to the rattle. Hanna felt as if it had a story to tell. Its first sounds created goose bumps on her skin, and her body resonated with the heartbeat rhythm that she instinctively shook.

Trudy commended her. "Ah, it's good to see you feel the voice of the rattle. I see that you let it play itself; you flow with its beat, and it flows with you. Very good, Hanna. Now I'd like you to dream about a dark storm; see the thunderclouds, hear the lightning bolts, and begin to rattle—bring in the light with the rattle. Remember the cracks of light you created with the crystals and use their paths; blend in the light with the rhythm, my dear. Now watch as the sun rises before your eyes and the dark clouds drift away."

Hanna bowed her head to Trudy. "Thank you, my teacher, my friend, my mother. You have been my mother, oh dear one. I am grateful and answer to you with my full intent to not only be your good student, but also to become my true self. I trust in you; thank you."

Hanna knew not where her words came from, but this dream they were in made her feel so full within, and words came to her like a tree full of ripe apples; she could decipher different perspectives.

"Trudy, we are jumping a hoop here, aren't we? Something very important is going to happen. What is it, Trudy?"

Trudy nodded and smiled but said nothing. Her chin said it all as she pointed it toward the ceremony and told Hanna with a quick glance to pay attention.

Hanna stood up and looked into the center, where the fire raged. She saw billows of smoke rising above it; they felt alive, and she stared more closely into them. She watched as her wolf appeared in the smoke and began to present a series of images of herself at different ages. She was young, she was a baby, and there she was with a cane in her hand and white hair. She saw a pregnant image of herself for a split second, and then she was holding a child.

Her wolf would appear from time to time and change the perspective; she would suddenly see herself through the eyes of another. She felt their fear and apprehension and knew how she could better connect. She learned to bend and flow while retaining the same intent; she found out where her lies were and what was true. She knew she still had work to do on herself but was full with her progress.

"Hmmmmm, yes, Hanna," said her wolf. "Hmmmmmm, you have many decades to be all of the dreams you see here; your lessons will lie in your deeds, as you are a ray of light in this life. May you forever project this on us. It's a simple task; be your light as you are."

"You mean I just have to be?"

"Yes, be what you are now. That may change. But now, just be you, and study well, young one; treasures await you at every turn. Margaret will always mirror another way. You complement each other, and you will enjoy meeting every ten years."

Nano turned and ran off, leaving Hanna with words that rang like sirens in her head. *Enjoy meeting every ten years.* "You mean...?" she shouted, but she knew that the wolf would not respond. He was gone, and she turned to Trudy, pleading.

Trudy looked away, ignoring Hanna's boring eyes. "Shhh, we are in a ceremony! Dream on, Hanna; all of the answers are inside of you."

Hanna lay back and tried to relax into a dream within the dream of the pond and remembered that she was still in the water.

"Remember, bend like a willow, flow with the river, remember, Hanna!" Nano whispered in her ear.

She was on the verge of panicking, and Trudy knew that she could drown; she wondered why Nano encumbered her with this while she was dreaming. Trudy brought her being out of meditation and picked up Hanna and brought her out of the water. She laid her gently on a blanket next to Margaret, who was still asleep.

Hanna woke up seconds later with a giant headache, still upset and heaving for air. She tried to stand up and fell back on the blanket.

Trudy patted her down and tried to keep her level. "Hanna, we are here with you."

"No, you're going to leave me for ten years, and you're going to take Margaret with you! I know it; I just do!"

Trudy calmly replied, "Hanna, did you ever think that maybe you will leave us? That maybe it will be your decision, your act of power? I think that wolf stirred you up in the dreamtime for a good reason! As you danced with the rattle, the wolf wanted to rattle you! You were too complacent. You see, in life we need friction in order to begin change."

"I don't want to change anything! My life is perfect!"

"Well, maybe that's the problem, dear child. Nano certainly has shaken you up enough. Let's see where you go with this."

"For one, Trudy, I don't like that Nano makes these decisions without consulting me. He thinks he can just throw me through things at his leisure. I am not here for him."

Nano came trotting back from wherever he'd been. "Aha!" he said, amused. "Did we shake you up a bit? Things not as peachy as you thought?" He leaped in the air over a bush, tore into the river up to his belly, and then came out and shook his water all over them. "Howwwl!" He was spirited and wild; Hanna didn't know what to make of it. Her argumentativeness had melted away at the sight of her wolf's power. Her questions answered with the push of a wave and a nudge from the furred one, she began to allow the events to fall into place and see what she would do with them.

"I'm just going to spend the next ten years studying. Then I'll go on digs and discover our source; maybe I'll find an ancient treasure and become a famous anthropologist."

Trudy asked her if she would stay in England.

"I'll stay here as long as it suits me."

"What about a husband and children?" Trudy asked.

Margaret stirred to the sound of the questions. "Who's getting married?" She lay on her side propping up her head and smiled. She felt like she'd slept a thousand years. She also remembered her dreams, and laughed as they drifted back.

"Sleep well, my dear?" Trudy asked.

Mar yawned and stretched. "I dreamed you were all underwater. Did you go somewhere without me?"

"It doesn't sound like we were without you, Mar. Did you come to that gathering through the water too?" Hanna responded.

"No, but I watched you. You came back in a big panic, and I kept on sleeping; it was strange."

"Nano had some news for us. Just when we were going to have some fun, he goes and tells me that we will go our separate ways again. For another ten years. Can you believe it? I was pretty upset."

"And now?" Mar asked.

"Now, I realize that we will only grow from it, and I learned that my objection is part of my shadow. That unwillingness to bend, to trust. I see that I can mistrust too, that I, too, don't always have it just the way I want it. I also discovered that I react to change."

Margaret lay on her back and looked at the blue sky and big puffy clouds. "So what is going to happen? What was Trudy saying about marriage?"

"Are you not both women? Don't you think about men? Funny that I have to bring it up with you." Trudy spoke to both girls, who sat up and looked at each other and burst into giggles.

"I don't know; we haven't even talked about it ourselves!" Hanna said. "I had a friend who was a boy in high school, but I never talked to him about anything, and we didn't even kiss. Here at uni, the blokes are nice, I suppose, but I don't really think about it, although that's all most of the other girls talk about."

Margaret spoke up. "There was this one doctor at the hospital who was cute. I don't know; I wonder why we don't have boyfriends. Should we? You don't have a husband, and you seem happy. Do we have to get married?"

"One day, ladies, you will see someone across the room, and your eyes will lock; or someone will introduce you to a man, and you will be swept off your feet from the energy between you."

Hanna bragged, "I've only felt that with you, Nano. So it's sacred!"

Trudy laughed. "That's true love, yes, and it is sacred. When you meet your mate and when you feel this energy, it will remind you somewhat of the energy of the shadow, because passion is rooted underground and flows from your shadow."

Hanna turned to her wolf again. "I only see light from you, Nano; I don't feel shadow."

Nano blew up in the air, his breath so hot, they could see it. Hanna felt something inside her change at the sight of his passion as he breathed his fire into the air. Her belly turned upside down, and her chest warmed; a brightness appeared in her cheeks. Mar watched both of them and burst out laughing, rolling all over the blanket. Her giggles ignited Hanna, and she broke from what seemed like a spell.

"Whoa! Wow, what was that?" Hanna squealed to Trudy, her eyes wide as rainbows

Arched lines appeared on Trudy's brow, and her jaw dropped. Trudy was decidedly serious about the situation. She gently calmed Hanna, stroking her head and shoulders. Then she gave her a wallop on the back and said sternly, "Never laugh at a man's passion in his face. He will either kill you or punish you for the rest of your life."

Hanna noticed that Nano was unchanged by her reaction and looked at Trudy, confused. "Why, what's the problem? Nano didn't seem to mind."

"Nano is pure spirit. He has no ego, my dear."

Hanna and Mar quietly pondered the experience as they began to pack up their picnic and sacred tools, putting everything into Trudy's bag that seemed to hold much more than it looked like it could. Each of them was in her own world, reexamining the sensations she'd felt in her body; Hanna's was sweaty and energized, but Mar was still giggling.

"I'd probably get myself killed. The thought of a man acting like Nano just did? That's the most ridiculous thing I've ever seen! Maybe this man thing just isn't for me. I never really had a dad, I never saw my mom with a man, and really, I don't care!" Margaret stepped up her march back to the house, the dogs following her closely. She took deep breaths and loved the smell of the roses she passed, mixed with rifts of manure drifting in from the fields over the hill.

Hanna and Trudy followed Mar. Hanna was revved. "I'm starving; let's get straight in the car and go into town for fish and chips!"

Trudy nodded, and smiled at the thought of fried fish with vinegar, just like she'd grown up on. She looked up as they approached the cottage, and her heart journeyed again, far away to a distant time in the same place, as she watched the smoke coming from the chimney on the same cottage that her father had built.

Chapter 8

The fish-and-chips shop was in the center of town, sandwiched between two bookshops. Hay-on-Wye's bookshops and festivals are world-renowned; it is literally considered the book capital of the world.

As they queued up down the block, the three women window-shopped. In one window there were old vintage classics, and in another there was a display that Trudy was suddenly drawn to. She rushed over and cried out like a hawk, "Here is the book I was telling you about! Glory be, here it is! Oh, and it's beautifully presented, don't you think?" Hanna and Margaret stopped in front of the window, while losing their place in the queue, and Trudy drew them into her ecstasy. "Will you look at that? I never... we will celebrate! Come, ladies, we will all go buy ourselves each a copy!"

The book was exclusively exhibited; the cover was orangey, with a picture of a woman on it. It had an enchanting title, and Hanna looked to Mar and said, "Look! *Medicine Woman*! Did you know, Mar, that's what Trudy is? Yes, she's a medicine woman. Wonder what this book is all about. Trudy, do you know this book? Sure looks like it."

"*Do I know this book?* This book is the beginning of a very old teaching coming back to us. This woman, the author, Lynn Andrews, is writing more books. She writes about her teachers, the Sisterhood of the Shields, and about modern-day shamanism. You could give it to your professors in London, Hanna. That'll teach them a thing or two! She will be a great teacher for our time, and what a miracle, here we are halfway across the world and *Medicine Woman* is on display as we go and eat fish and chips! Divine..." She faded off and refocused on the fish-and-chips queue.

As they entered, the aroma of frying and vinegar enveloped them, and the sound of the boiling oil and the shouts between chef and cashier overwhelmed them. It felt like another world to Trudy, who kept falling back to another time.

Then she saw him—his shadow, his sideburns, his square shoulders. She saw the girls too and wasn't sure which time she was in.

Hanna elbowed her when they reached the counter, and Trudy ordered for all three of them with a robotic voice; she looked vacant. Hanna became slightly concerned. "Trudy? Are you okay?" She touched her arm gently. Trudy ignored her and seemed focused on someone in the crowd.

The chippie served up the food, and they gathered it and walked into the street to find a place to eat. The evening was warm, and they found tables right outside. Trudy was distant and kept turning around, as if looking for someone. Then the oddest thing happened. A strange handsome man dressed in period clothing, almost costume-like, approached their table and stood in front of Trudy, bearing down on her with a smile that infected them all. Margaret and Hanna burst into giggles as Trudy looked up at her pursuer.

"Well, I'll be...!" she said in delight; her eyes awoke and sparkled little drops of glee around her. Trudy stood and embraced the young man; their reunion brought tears to all eyes. Mar and Hanna sat quietly as the two reacquainted. Sniffing each other like wolves, they circled, they hugged, they stepped back and gazed at each other. It was a dance of two; each reflecting each other's movements and attraction, and then backing away in awe.

Hanna became impatient with the dance and butted in. "Trudy, would you like to introduce us to your friend?"

The man addressed the girls for the first time. He looked over at them and gazed with pride. "Oh, aren't you two a pair of pretty ones? I will be pleased to find suitors for you! You know, for some it's hard when they don't possess the aesthetic finesse, but you two are natural beauties—your manners so true. Hmmm..." He looked and considered them, sizing them up.

"Hanna and Margaret, I'd like to introduce you to an old friend of mine. He seems to have never grown up, but he has chosen to appear to us in this way. I met him when I was your age, and he drew me close to him. Aaron, these are my two apprentices. How fortunate we are to meet you here! Are you visiting, or do you still live here?"

Aaron spoke slowly, with a very different accent. They moved in to hear and understand his words. They were not familiar with his dialect, and hesitant.

"Ahhhhh, Trudy, true woman of the elk and the sea, such a fortunate day it is to meet you here! Ahhh, and what have we here, did you say? Apprentices? Margaret and Hanna, I am honored to meet your acquaintance." He bowed slightly to them.

They squirmed in their seats, and the giggling resumed. Both were flushed at their cheeks and kicked each other under the table. How they wished they could slide straight under and peek up at him from the safety of the floor. He felt so strong. They were not familiar with this kind of person.

"That's because he isn't a person, darling," Trudy said to Mar. She cupped her hand over Mar's warm cheek to cool it. "You are witnessing a bridging of the times. This man is not of our time; he is part of my memory. It is a very strong memory for me and has physically manifested itself here with us. The other people cannot see him, only us. So we should be discreet."

Hanna tugged at Trudy. "I don't understand, Trudy, how do you know him?"

"Well, my daughter, I grew up here. I found it very interesting when you chose to come here for the summer; my journey was very powerful, and the memory still lives within me. I never extinguished the fire of my first love; the energy served me in my work, and I loved reminiscing. It is part of your journey now, too, as you chose to come here. Isn't that right, Aaron? What do you have to share with my two apprentices?"

"I think I have the perfect gift for you, my ladies. Will you both accompany me to the summer ball this evening at the castle?"

"Summer ball? Do we have to dress in those awful Victorian dresses? I mean, I don't mind going, but I'm not very refined for a castle," Hanna said.

Margaret was not enthused with the idea. "I don't know how to dance."

"Who's going to be there anyway?" Hanna asked Trudy.

"Ladies, we are very fortunate to be here for this magnificent ball! I remember it fondly, Aaron. The girls have nothing to wear; will you take them for fittings?"

"Yes, of course. Finish up your food. Fittings on full bellies, hmmm," he reconsidered. "The ball begins in only a few hours; no time to digest. My apologies; you'll have to skip dinner. These corsets will have you holding your breath for relief!"

"Did you say corsets? I think not, sir. This isn't the fourteenth century!" Margaret protested.

"Oh, but it is at the ball, my dear. Didn't Trudy explain to you where you are?"

Mar and Hanna stared at Trudy accusingly, brows arched to both their noses on faces with pouted lips.

She turned away and held her hand to her mouth, trying to hide her smile and chuckle. "Yes, girls, I told you this is the magical world of Wyrrd, where anything *could* happen… I suppose I neglected to tell you that the rules of time don't always apply in these parts, and you can find pockets of the past and the future sitting in the present for all to see but only few to access. You are chosen to access, and I will prepare you enough; but first go and get fitted and come back to the cottage. I will have a ceremony ready for you, and then we will all go to the ball!"

They agreed to follow Aaron in Hanna's car and drop Trudy off at the cottage first. On the way, they had more time to question Trudy about the time warp she'd told them about.

"Okay, Trudy, what is really happening? Is this guy for real? I mean, where did he pop up from, and how did we just 'change' times when everything else is the same?" Margaret asked.

"I promise you the ball won't be 'the same,' child. I ask you to soak your spirit in the spring and be supple; be in trust, my ladies. Observe and witness. Be grateful."

They had reached the cottage and dropped off Trudy.

Aaron left his car in the driveway and joined them in Hanna's car. "I'll sit in the front and direct you," he said.

"You can drive if you want, sir. I prefer to sit in the back anyway." Hanna offered him the wheel and opened the back door to sit down. "As you wish," he said and sat down in the driver's seat.

Before he set off, he tried to put them both at ease. "I know this must seem like a dream to you, and in essence it is a dream, just like anything else, but tonight you will experience another time. Today you will be fitted with the clothes so that you will fit in and be comfortable, as if you are also in another time. Which you are."

Mar and Hanna were even more perplexed than before, and Hanna grabbed Margaret's elbow from the side of her seat.

"Stop worrying, ladies," Aaron said. "You are going to have a wonderful time. When you choose your dress, choose something that will allow you to feel your truth, which will comfort you at the ball. Apart from the corsets, the dresses are most magnificent! They have the best silks and linen; the wool is always soft. You will love it, and the dressers will treat you well."

Aaron finished just as they pulled up at a building that looked like it had fallen out of the sky from the fifteenth century. It was all gray stone, bound together with black mud; the walls round it were over twenty feet tall, and the gate was heavy. Aaron held it open for them, and they entered into a courtyard of cobblestone and a vegetable and herb garden. They inhaled the wonderful aromas from the garden and walked into the ancient house smiling.

The entryway had a few chairs, and they sat down and waited to be helped. Moments later, a very, very small man came into the hallway for them. He was dressed like a tailor, black suit and tape measure round his neck. He led them into a large room with gilded ceilings and tall, open windows, which stood twenty feet from the floor.

There was plenty of light for fittings, and the room was set up by what looked like periods to the girls. There was women's wear from every century since the beginning of time, they thought, and at first just reveled in the history and studying each time period. Aaron kept urging them to choose something to leave time for the tailor to make the adjustments, but the girls were enjoying their first shopping spree too much to pay much attention to him.

Then Hanna saw her dress. She stood before it for a few moments, gently touching each strand, each little bead and crystal securely sewn into the material. She couldn't imagine actually wearing it! It was made of an off-white doeskin with silk lining; the top bodice was a corset of bending bones, which allowed her to breathe while it held close to her skin. The full long skirt fell to the floor in pleats, and an accordion-folded edge kept it from touching the floor. The beads and stones were hand-sewn onto the doeskin with sheer silk draping over the top, making a three-dimensional fabric. One would have thought that the doeskin would make it heavy, but when Hanna tried it on, it fit like a glove and moved with each shift of her body.

"How does it feel?" Margaret asked. "You should be comfortable."

"I can't even feel it on! Only the softness of the suede, that is all I feel. Oh, and tingling all over—is that from all the crystal beads?"

Aaron stood back and looked at her. He was aghast at her beauty and her naïveté. Margaret had a dark shadow that he could see and relate to, but Hanna—her light just slipped through his fingers like an infinite game of cat and mouse between their energies.

Hanna felt her Nano's presence with her every move. He licked her doeskin with approval.

"You need some moccasins. Come, the shoes are over there. Let's go find you some, and then we'll work with Margaret," Aaron said, noting that she had not yet seen anything she was attracted to.

"Hanna, you look lovely!" Mar told her after she'd found some beige soft lamb's wool-lined moccasins. They had no soles, and she would only wear them indoors.

Aaron led Margaret over to another section. It was more of a crafty, peasantry style; the clothes were displayed on hooks hung on the walls of wooden log cabins, and tall trees grew in between the aisles. Peasant tops and skirts hung from tree branches, and Mar suddenly spied a long gown in a rustic color, not orange, not brown, more golden with blood-orange highlights. She reached up and touched it, discovering that it was a combination of silk and embroidered net. Like Hanna's, it was adorned with crystal beads and symbols sewn into the fabric, but on Mar's, the stones reflected off the darker color. When Margaret tried it on, the colors twinkled and reflected from her curves to the walls of the room.

"Margaret, you are like a disco ball! What are they, sequins you have? Mine isn't as sparkly as yours!" Hanna offered.

Aaron interjected, "Do not compare, as each is made for each of you. You were attracted to them because they were meant for you. Don't compare and regret, or question and deject. Wear your dress in pride and joy; wear it as you would wear yourself. This ball will change you, adjust you, mature you. Roll with this ball, my ladies."

Margaret did a little twirl with her full skirt and cried out laughing, "Look, watch me twirl! This is fun!"

Hanna came over, and they twirled together. Mocking a waltz, they joined hands and pranced around the room.

Margaret chose some blue pumps to wear with her dress. They felt like magic slippers, the insides so soft, and she knew she would fly in them if she asked.

When they returned to the cottage, Trudy had the back garden set up for a ceremony. Somehow, she had transformed the back patio into an overgrown vineyard, whose vines climbed on fencing, creating a gazebo-type structure where she had set up a couple of altars and laid blankets on the ground.

Mar and Hanna were instructed to sit on the blanket close to a pile of gourds that Trudy had strategically placed on the western side of the circle. They each picked up a gourd and began to inspect it, raising their heads to Trudy inquisitively, only to be silenced by her eyes. They sat in compliance with whole heart awaiting her next move.

Aaron had gone into the house, and they didn't feel the presence of the wolves. They were alone with Trudy.

She walked around them a couple of times, her hand busy smudging as she passed. She was in a trancelike state, and the two simply sat and felt her. She brought a calm wind into the circle, which they both acknowledged as they felt its velvet brush by their cheeks, wiping all concern from them and leaving them open to her story.

She looked up to the sky and began to sing like a bird, her high treacle pitched off the ceiling, and the girls could feel its light and its joy. It was a courting tune she sang, and the girls giggled. Trudy sat down in the center of the circle and faced them in the west. She took a gourd to her hand and held it to her nose, sniffing the sweetness. Then without saying a word, she grabbed a large knife and thrust it into the gourd, chopping it in two halves. Hanna and Mar looked at the two sides parted, revealing the orange-colored meat and seeds. The girls gasped at her strength. Trudy took one half and set it aside. The she took a spoon to the other half and scooped out its seeds and placed them aside. Then she scraped the inside and removed the remaining meat.

Trudy stated solemnly, "This gourd represents your emptiness and your fullness. Tonight you will experience being filled with a new emotion. I would like you to imagine that you are tiny and can fit in this beautiful gourd. Imagine that the orange walls are crystalline and each rock is soft to touch and safe to eat. In here, imagine that this is your womb, your place of recreation, your place that awakens from love and ecstasy. See yourselves in harmony in this place, your gourd of love. You may call it your sacred gourd. In the coming days we will work with her, and tonight before you go to your first ball, I am introducing you to her so that you may find a place within you for her teachings, her receptivity; she has come to change you."

Trudy stood up and circled the girls again. They sat quietly, inspecting the two halves of the gourd, one carved and hollow, one fertile and full of meat and seeds. They took both and imprinted their shapes on the ground. They held them to their noses and smelled their essence. Mar and Hanna began to feel different and suddenly serious.

"Trudy, are we really going to meet our mates tonight?" Hanna asked, feeling slightly excited and totally terrified at the idea. "I don't know if I even want a husband, Trudy. Who is this guy anyway, from the past, trying to be a matchmaker or something? It's so old-fashioned. Ya know?"

Margaret nodded in agreement. "Yeah, this gourd thing. You say it's a symbol of my womb? Well, I kinda want to keep mine empty. No babies for me!"

"Trudy!" they called out in unison, and Trudy turned and scowled at them like they were naughty children. "Be patient; open and flow with this, my dears." That was all she said, and the following uncomfortable moments passed very, very slowly. They saw something happen as Trudy continued to circle them. It was all appearing in their clear view; they couldn't touch it, but it was happening. A man and a woman were circling each other. They were courting, and then dancing and then intertwined into each other.

As Hanna and Margaret watched the dance between the male and the female, they began to feel more balanced within their own bellies. Each of them settled a bit and continued to watch the vision. The man and the woman had totally merged, and their energy pulsated so impeccably that Margaret and Hanna began to dance and cajole with each other in the physical.

Trudy laughed to herself; she half expected to find them attracted to each other. *All the more reason to take them to the ball; let them be aware of their choices for love on earth.* Neither was brought up with conditioning to settle down and have babies, yet society still expected it. Trudy knew she had to expose them to the norm of family. If even in this unconventional way.

Nano swiped her across her head as she struggled with her responsibility. "Don't worry so, dear one. Hanna and Mar will find their way. They have us inside of them too. We are not celibate, and neither will they be. You guided Hanna well. Margaret is catching up, getting filled with love. That's what she needs right now. Trudy, you do well," he stated finely and gave her another nudge with his nose, pushing her over into Hanna, who was standing in her place in the west still, feeling Nano's presence.

"Trudy!" she cried. "Was that my wolf?"

"Yes, Hanna, he was here for a moment to give me guidance."

"You need guidance? I thought you knew everything, Trudy," Margaret said.

Trudy stroked Margaret's head and held her to her breast for a moment. "You precious spirit, you..." she whispered, and kissed the top of her head.

Margaret asked, "Can we get dressed now? Is it nearly time to go?"

"Oh, so you are excited now?" Trudy asked.

"Yes, I am. I feel much better; I feel excited. Who knows? Maybe I will meet a man. Seems unlikely, but who knows?" Margaret smiled and laughed to Hanna.

Hanna was less enthusiastic, yet she had loosened up some too. "Yes, let's get this thing over with. Maybe it'll be fun."

Aaron was driving Hanna's car, and the three women were packed into the backseat. There was a magnificent seven-layer cake occupying the front passenger seat. Trudy kind of came up with it just as they finished getting ready and were getting into the car. It smelled freshly baked, and the girls wanted a taste.

"Come on," they teased her. "You can fix it up with the stroke of your will anyway. Can't we have a piece? Oh please?"

"There will be a feast when we arrive; don't fill up on cake now."

As they drove through town, Aaron, at the wheel, pointed to the gray castle, which was over on the other side of the river at the foot of one of the Black Mountain foothills. The old bridge was still working; they crossed over at sunset and were all mesmerized by the view.

There seemed to be a mist that floated into the car and the view; they all heard the same fluttering of wings, and angelic-voiced choirs consumed their beings. They were no longer in a car but on a golden gilded carriage, sitting on red velvet plush seats, peering out of wide-open windows at the green hills empty of modern telephone poles and asphalt roads. The castle was in clear view, and they approached it on a cobblestone road, which was lined with children waving flags and dancing to the music that blared out from the castle grounds.

There was an air of festivity, and Hanna, Margaret, and Trudy stepped out of the carriage with Aaron's help and skipped up the stairs leading up into the castle's entrance. Bugles sounded with their arrival, and the girls looked round to see who had arrived, only to find everyone cheering them.

"Trudy, why are they cheering us?" Margaret asked.

"They are making you welcome, dear ladies. This is your coming-out party!"

"Coming out to what?" Hanna asked indignantly. "Where are we going?"

"You are being introduced to an older time, ladies, just like the teachings in the books that Lynn Andrews is writing. Like the teachings from her book, here you are actually living in the old time for this party. You will be given the gift of seeing life from the other side, as they say."

"What? From the past, like the dead? I don't get it," Margaret protested.

"Trudy, what is happening?" asked Hanna.

The two looked around them. They could feel they were in another time; it smelled different, and it tasted different. Their bellies felt stupefied by butterflies, and their minds were beginning to feel like mush.

"I'm getting a headache!" Margaret complained as she noticed that all of the people were dressed like her and were carrying trays and trays of food into a grand banquet room that they soon entered. The abundance was overwhelming for Margaret; she'd never seen so much food in her life. It seemed unreal to her, and maybe it was. "Trudy, my head really hurts here." She went and latched her arm round Trudy's. "Can we go? I don't like this feeling in my body."

"Dear one, please try and quiet yourself and allow the love of this time and place to enter you. Remember the gourd; let it inside your gourd," Trudy said.

Hanna walked close to Margaret and led her to a seat at a table in the banquet room. Everyone was starting to sit down, and the food looked so tempting. The tables soon filled, and the crowd suddenly became very quiet.

At the front of the room, a tall woman stood. Her long hair was black and silver streaked and dropped down her back; she had black eyes, and their stare penetrated Hanna and Margaret. They drew in a nervous breath, but then a bright smile appeared on her face and the girls could practically feel the love from her smile. They warmed and yearned to approach her, though Trudy gave them a look and they stayed in their seats. The woman stood up in front of the entire crowd and welcomed Hanna and Margaret to their circle. She said that they were the future of the circle and congratulated Trudy on her guardianship.

Mar and Hanna felt good and strong. This strange and beautiful woman, almost a goddess, was at first startling with her stare, but then she became so warm and welcoming.

Nano laughed and gave Hanna a shove in the back, nearly tipping over her glass.

"Nano!" Hanna whispered.

"You don't have to whisper here, dear Hanna. You are in your circle; you don't have to hide here."

"Where am I, Nano?"

"You are in the dreamtime, but you are still on earth."

"How's that?"

"Well, if you were to suddenly 'fall' out of this dream, you would still be at the castle, and there is a party in the castle tonight in the physical. It may not be your kind of party, but there is a party here tonight in all the times."

Margaret said, "Why was that woman so threatening one minute and welcoming the next? She had me so taken back by her stare, and then she smiled and love just sank right into me! It was amazing!"

Nala responded, "Remember the gourd, child; she make you open up to receive her love. You see?"

"Hmmmmm." Margaret turned to Hanna, grabbed both of her hands, and jumped in her seat. "You know, Hanna, I keep thinking we're going to wake up and discover this is all a dream."

The food was being served, and they settled in for the feast. There was turkey and rabbit stew. Large turkey drumsticks were served with silk napkins as holders; the potatoes were roasted to perfection. The four of them were silent for the duration of the meal. Looks were exchanged, approving each course—the ladies were in gastro heaven—and the silent eating continued until after the last chocolate mousse serving had gone. They sat silly from food, sipping wine and beer.

The goddess woman was speaking of them again, and their attention moved to the top of the room. She was talking to Trudy, asking her to bring Margaret and Hanna up to the front of the room for their welcoming ceremony. The girls did not yet know, but they were about to personally meet everyone at the ball. They looked so beautiful, both of them with their new gowns and glittery jewelry.

Aaron beamed with pride as he and Trudy walked them up to the head of the tables, where there were two grand chairs, throne-like with soft plush red velvet seats. Hanna and Margaret were asked to sit on them and heard the goddess woman announce, "Gentlefolk, stewards of the forests, the lakes, the mountains, and the underworld, we gather here today to celebrate the merging of the times, the summer fest of love where we meet once a decade. And this year I am proud to introduce our guests of honor, who will now receive you and all of your blessings."

Margaret and Hanna held court nestled in their comfy chairs. Each party approached them with honor and a warm love that they received gracefully. The two were a picture of poise and perfection in their manner; Trudy stood tall with pride. After about an hour, they became restless. Trudy suspended the procession to allow Hanna and Margaret to mingle a bit and move around. On their path through the crowd, they noticed people who had not been introduced to them. They looked different, although neither of them could figure out what it was.

A Wolf Song

Margaret noticed a man sitting at the edge of the balcony that opened out into the back courtyard leading from the banquet room. She found herself alone; Hanna must have stopped to chat. Her curiosity lured her to the shadowy side of the balcony where he sat. He was gazing over to a tree on the grass nearby and hadn't paid the least attention to Margaret, who was now approaching him. Margaret felt the snugness of her dress; the silk lining felt like a glove holding her softly, and she could sense her body as she looked over at him.

She wondered what it was he was looking at and tried to move in close undetected to see the tree. Something was rustling in the leaves, and then she saw a great brown and rustic colored bird. It must have been over a foot tall, and its wings looked like they could stretch out a yard at least.

"Excuse me, sir, but what kind of bird is that?" Margaret said quietly so as not to startle him, though she did anyway.

He jumped, and so did the bird. None too pleased, he turned to Margaret and sneered, "Well, thanks a lot, you scared the poor one away!"

Margaret tried to be as polite as she could. "I'm ever so sorry, sir. I didn't realize..." she trailed off, gazing into his angry eyes.

They began to soften as he looked at her and her dress and blue shoes; his eyes rested there. "Are you going to tap your heels and take off somewhere? Those look like flying shoes to me," he said.

Margaret laughed and agreed. "Yeah, me too. I thought that when I got them. I haven't tried them out yet. Would you like me to try them out and go and find your bird for you?" she teased. "What kind of bird was that anyway? He was huge!"

"That's what you Americans call a buzzard; we call it an eagle here." He said, noting her American accent.

"That was an eagle?" Margaret gasped. She turned to search for Hanna to tell her but couldn't see her inside. "I gotta go," she said to the man.

"Not so quick, young lady. You interrupted me and my bird flew off, and you're not even going to introduce yourself?"

Margaret stopped and turned to him, blushing brightly. His attention seemed to fill her with goose bumps, and she couldn't lose the grin on her face. "Oh, sorry, I'm Margaret. My friend Hanna is inside. We came with Trudy and Aaron. Do you know them?"

"Oh, so you are the guest of honor! I never go on those processions where you spent most of the ball, I reckon. Prefer myself to wait and see if I meet you without the formalities. And see, we did. Margaret, I will come and introduce myself to your party."

"How about you introduce yourself to me first?"

The gentlemen, who was in his mid twenties, had sandy ginger tousled hair covering his ears and forehead and sticking off his collar. He was dressed from another time again. Not quite Victorian, but later, perhaps World War II workingman's dress. A nice jacket, white shirt, shiny shoes, but no top hat nor tails.

Margaret dared to ask him, "I know why you didn't come to introduce yourself. You are not of this time, are you? It's okay; neither am I. But I think I'm in the present and you are in the past. Right?"

He turned to Margaret and answered, "This is a carnival of all times together, and time does not really exist here. There is a very particular circle of folk who are welcoming you here tonight. Who brought you? Didn't they tell you?"

"I told you. I came here with Aaron—don't you know him?" Margaret asked. "Yeah, I get why we're here." She paused and blushed slightly, looking down and then up at the man's face. She said quietly, "I think we're supposed to meet men here. Although I'm not looking for a boyfriend or anything, but I think that's the general idea." She considered telling him about the ceremony with the gourd but decided to keep it to herself.

"You still haven't shared your name with me." Margaret got up and stood over him with her hands on her hips. Then she turned and looked for Hanna again; surely she must be coming out soon, and she wanted Hanna to meet this man. "You want to dance?"

"My name is Rupert Crowley. I have lived here, and I live here again. I am the keeper of this castle. It is not of our custom for a lady to ask a man to dance, but I suppose you are just ignorant and not being forward with me." He stood in front of her, and she gazed into his eyes and felt captivated by their light. There was a twinkle in his eye, and she could almost see herself in the reflection. He held his hand out to her. "May I have this dance?"

"Dance? Now? I can't right now, I have to find my friend, come with me." Margaret grabbed his hand without waiting for his response and led him into the banquet room to look for Hanna. The banquet was in full swing, the music and dim lights obstructed Margaret's view and she began to doubt she could find Hanna in the crowd. She stood still for a moment, still clutching Ruperts wrist and shut her eyes. She asked Nala to lead them to Hanna and Trudy. Nala jumped at the opportunity to help her, and Margaret wove through the crowd, trusting that she would soon bump into her.

They walked all the way through the dance floor and past the food into another, smaller room. It was like a library but had been set up like a painter's class, with chairs and easels that were full of people all working on their own paintings. They all had their pallet of magnificent color in one hand and brush in the other. There was a feeling of creativity in the air, and Margaret could hear a minstrel song in the background. She listened intently and then spotted Hanna, Trudy, and Aaron; there was someone else with them too.

After they approached the small group, Margaret asked, "Aaron, do you know Rupert?" Margaret looked shyly over at the other individual; he looked familiar somehow, but she didn't know him. Margaret looked at all of the paintings and absorbed the music, her heart filling; she felt complete. She listened briefly to the minstrel's meandering tune, accompanied by his mandolin:

> There once was a young one, who'd never been kissed,
> She got to thinkin' it over, what she had missed.
> She got her a guy and then she kissed him and all,
> And Uh-oh, she kissed him again.
> He had kisses sweeter than wine; he had...

Suddenly Margaret stood before the crowd. Her soprano voice was steady and in tune. She listened to herself as everyone else stopped their painting and turned their attention to her.

> There once were two girls named Mar and Hanny,
> And we met by the side of the tall alder tree.
>
> We looked in the river, and we climbed down its banks
> Till there up before us stood two wolves, smart as snakes.

And Trudy, our keeper, who we hold so dear,
Make it clear, make it clear,
Make my fear disappear!

Trudy brushed a tear from her eye and looked up at Margaret, moving toward her to give her a hug.

Hanna also set down her paints and ran over to her. "Mar, that was beautiful! This is the creativity room. Do you want to paint? Look at mine!" She pulled her over to her easel. Hanna had painted a landscape of mountains and farmland, very much like their surroundings at the cottage.

Mar loved it and said, "Hanna, can I take that back to the States with me? I want it always."

"What do you mean, go back to the States?" Hanna asked.

"Well, I'm going to have to go back at one point and figure out what I'm going to do with my life. I can't live here. You will go back to London at the end of the summer, to school, and I can't go to school. I don't even have a high school diploma. Maybe that's what I should do."

"Trudy, can Mar live with you?" Hanna asked.

Trudy responded, "Ladies, is the time for this discussion now and here?" She looked around; the people were back at their paintings, and the minstrel had resumed his song. "I would love to have Margaret live with me; of course, you are welcome, my child."

Mar said, "So, good; it's settled. I'll go live with Trudy, and Hanna, you'll come to visit. Okay?"

Chapter 9

Trudy and Aaron were sitting in the corner of the room away from Mar and Hanna and Rupert, who were all busy painting. Finally alone, they could steal a few moments to themselves. Words served no purpose as the two gazed into each other's eyes with silly grins, each in his or her own dream, yet deeply connected.

Nala studied them, knowing they could read each other's thoughts, and by their body language, they were clearly communicating. They were in another time, another plane. She circled them from above and held their space for them in her womb and in her heart. She was assisting them with their celestial travel in between time and space. She held it in her belly and in her heart. She cocooned them, and with her protection, they felt bold enough to speak.

"Trudy, dear one, elk spirit, come to me. Bring forth your story. Oh, I love thee so." Aaron spoke in a kindly tune-like dialect, and Nala swayed with its melody. "My dear long-lost love," he sang to her, and she smiled quietly, peacefully, filling herself with his light and his love.

She sang sweetly to herself, and soon enough her voice filled the room. She sang a ballad of many verses, its beginning before time and its end after. Her song captivated everyone in the room, and a joyous chorus was repeated again and again:

> Our lifetimes collide like stars,
> Sparking fire and smoking out pain
> Of past lives all gone by. Let them sway, let them pray, let them stay
> With us for all times for all seasons.
> My spark, your smoke,
> We speak.

Her tones resonated throughout the room, where the people, as if hypnotized, filed away from their paintings and into a large circle of dance and song. Aaron sat and watched his love of then and now. He waited again, as Trudy received grace from the people and Hanna and Margaret joined in her celebration. He thought, *an interesting teaching*; here he was again sitting in the background, watching his love bask in glory and love. He suddenly realized after lifetimes of lessons the reason why they never could be together. This powerful medicine woman could not share her life with a man; she was married to her path.

He joined her in the center of the circle and held her, and she received him. He whispered in her ear, "You are free of me, loved one; I free you from my pursuit forever."

Trudy was startled by his words and looked at him questioningly.

He kissed her forehead and then took her hand and kneeled before her. "From this day forward, walk with my love in your heart and your soul; take my love and spread it as you know how. I no longer ask of you, dear sweet Trudy."

"Aaron, my honor for you is more the stronger with your love in me. I welcome you into my spirit always and am honored to receive you. My gratitude for the freedom you offer is infinite, Aaron. You give me freedom, and I return it with love from the universe, in three dimensions, over a hundred lifetimes. You fill me."

It was time to leave the ball. Their experience having been so surreal, Hanna half expected a giant pumpkin carriage to take them home. She had stopped questioning and simply accepted the strange people and things they had seen. Margaret was exhausted and grabbed Hanna's hand as they left; she was asleep before the car left the parking.

Going home, Hanna drove, and Aaron went home by himself. He and Trudy had said their farewells. Aaron realized he wasn't going to match her girls up with anyone and teased them when they parted, saying, "Well, young maidens, I see that you too are already married to your paths." They asked what path he was referring to, and he laughed and turned to Trudy with trust in his voice and said, "Ah, dear Trudy, have you not given them their power words yet? They know not who they are yet?"

Trudy responded with smiles and hugs, her silence stating everything. All in good time, they knew.

In the days that followed, the three—Trudy, Margaret, and Hanna, witnessed by their wolves and other deities—sat with the new book they had purchased in town the afternoon before the ball, *Medicine Woman*. They took turns reading it aloud as they busied their hands with herbs that Trudy gave them each day. She'd instructed them to work with the plants, to look at them and learn their attributes and what they had to say. She'd taught them some meditation techniques and offered them gateways in their dreams where, when passed, they could see the life in all. This enabled them to communicate with the herbs, while listening or reading the story of Lynn Andrews, her teachers, and the lesson of Red Dog and the marriage basket. The girls were fascinated with the story, and Trudy was inclined to pull them back and balance it with her own metaphorical teachings.

Nano and Nala played with them while they read the book. Oftentimes, Hanna and Mar would find themselves watching visuals of the story, and they knew that the wolves were streaming the visions to them. They began to suspect that the wolves knew this story already; they showed them things that were yet to happen in the book. When they came upon it in the book, Mar and Hanna would stop in astonishment as they read whole paragraphs that they *knew* they'd heard before.

It was during these serendipitous episodes that they began to realize how life with these teachings was becoming a period of remembering and forgetting. Reading *Medicine Woman* was shifting their perspective of life, and their changes were quickened to lightning speed. At times, it was abrupt and upsetting, and they each spent time with the grief, the misunderstandings of youth and losses they had endured. These journeys always ended with some kind of joy. Trudy would somehow pull them out of the depths of their pain by dropping slight hints and baiting them toward the light. Margaret and Hanna always took the bait of love.

"Trudy, do you remember my dad, Jay? Didn't he seem like Red Dog? Could it be that everyone has a red dog?" Hanna asked one day while they were lounging on blankets under the alder trees lining the riverbank.

It was cool, and the sky, sparkling blue, hosted clouds the shape of huge pumpkins as the sun shone brightly through them.

Trudy focused on one of the alder tree branches that were drooping down close to the ground. She could feel the dark vindictive energy that cumulated in the shadow of the branches, and her face creased as she looked up at the girls and, seething, said, "Youuu seeee, you feel this junk, you feel like a lead weight within you when you dwell on his darkness, Hanna? You can feel it. Let it go through you, and then give it to the earth, where it will be cleansed. Isn't that what Agnes has been teaching Lynn? When you consider Jay and the energy that he held, it is only a teaching for you. So if you ever see it again, you will recognize it before it tries to kill you!"

Trudy's words saddened Hanna. "I wish I could feel good about Jay one day. He is my father."

"Hanna, that may be one of your biggest lessons in this lifetime. Margaret, who is the red dog in your life?"

"Oh, nobody. I only have to fear myself," she said. "I am my own red dog. In my life, I haven't coped very well with my fears nor with my aspirations, but now I am learning to identify the red dogs within me, the way I let myself get out of hand and I really become insane. Trudy, I think I will be balanced someday. As for Red Dog, he isn't as scary to me as he is to you, Hanna."

"We haven't finished the book yet; let's see what happens," Trudy said.

Nala howled into the sky, and in her breath, the girls could see Lynn crawling through a forest with a basket in her hand. They both looked at each other and Trudy too. Then, the two offered tobacco and sweet grass to their wolves and all of the deities around them; so full of gratitude they were, that the tears of joy flowed and they sang to release the emotion, the deeply overwhelming feeling of what they had experienced from the teachings in *Medicine Woman*.

"Trudy, when can we meet this Lynn Andrews? We need to work with her, I think," Hanna said.

Trudy laughed with delight. "Yes, indeed, my daughters!" She put her arms round them both and said, "Someday you will. Someday you will be thankful for the strength that you built, for learning to be physically strong enough to face every challenge. You are on the very first step of your enlightenment, dear lovely young women. You will both be very powerful in your lives. Margaret, we will rely on you for your insights of what will be; and Hanna, we will always know that you speak divine truth and vulnerability; your essence reflects this, and someday you will learn to live in this God-given skin."

She continued as the soft breeze blew over them, and the world could not have been more perfect. "We will be departing from this sacred ground soon. Hanna, you will go back to school, and your life will be full of adventures of past lives as you dig with your shovel into the past lives, both physical and spiritual. I know you will continue reading Lynn as she writes more books and that you will challenge your conditioning and your schooling with the wisdom that you glean from it. Margaret, you will come back with me to my stone house on the corner, and will finish your high school and get your diploma. After that, see what you want to study. We will meet again in ten years as our wolves demand, in trust and vulnerability.

Jay Templeton had been committed at King's County Mental Hospital for a good ten years, and his rehabilitation was almost complete. Going on eight years back one of the therapists had introduced art therapy into the program, and Jay began to paint. From the day he put brush to canvas, something inside opened up, and at first his memory returned. His deep psychosis had wiped out all memory of the horrifying night ten years earlier when he had massacred his family, leaving Hanna for dead in the front yard. As the memories returned to him, Jay channeled all of his emotion through his painting and created breathtaking pieces.

Unbeknown to Hanna, he had been selling his paintings for vast amounts of money, and apart from paying his hospital stay, the funds were being held for her in a trust. The trustee was appointed by the courts, as there was no one to contact. But Jay had insisted that the funds be held for Hanna. He knew he had a daughter and wanted somehow to make her life better. He held no hope that she would ever forgive him, but paying her way gave him a satisfaction and filled him with the motivation to paint and earn money for her. He also assumed that he would never be released from this place and that he could not afford to be completely sane as they could put him in a real prison for the rest of his days.

Over the course of Hanna's studies, one of her projects involved creating a family tree and researching her own genealogy. She knew that the only living relative she knew of was Jay, and it was at this time that she happened to be chatting with Trudy on the telephone about him and her project. "Trudy, do you think you could contact Riverpark and see if he's still there? I would like to interview him about our ancestors and Mom's and find out if I have any aunts and uncles, because I don't remember any relatives ever!"

"Hanna, I can call Riverpark and make some inquiries, but this is your project. You should approach him, not me.," was Trudy's response.

"Sure, I will, but maybe you could get it off the ground?" Hanna asked, hoping.

"Hanna, this is your act of power. I know I said that I would call Riverpark, but on second thought, I think you should. Here is the telephone number…" Trudy said as she flipped through her old tattered book of addresses. It was falling apart, but she knew exactly where the number was listed and she dictated it out to Hanna.

"Okay, okay, just a moment. I have to get a pen. Wait, will you?"

Trudy chuckled as she could feel the power of this mission moving from her to Hanna, who was now becoming an adult. She was so proud.

Margaret got up from her studies and took the phone from Trudy. "If this means you're coming home for a visit, then I think it's a good idea, whatever you are talking about! What's all this about Riverpark?" Mar's memories of the place were not fond, and the sound of the word made her shudder.

Trudy hushed her and read out the number again to Hanna. She hung up and told Mar to go back to her homework.

Hanna checked the time difference and decided it was now or never. She plucked up every inch of her strength, closed her eyes, and saw Nano standing by her side; she brushed her cheek against his fur and felt his heat. It fueled her courage as she heard the line begin to ring.

"Good morning, Riverpark," a woman's voice stated politely on the other end.

Hanna's heart raced as she asked the vital question. "Um, hi, um, do you have a patient named Jay Templeton?"

There was silence on the other end. The woman was taken back slightly as she had never had a request for this patient and had never expected to. She knew he'd killed his family, she knew about Hanna, and she knew it was Hanna on the other end of the line.

Hanna became impatient. "Hello? Is there anybody there?"

"Oh yes, yes, so sorry, ma'am. Did you say Jay Templeton?"

"Yes, I did. Is he there? This is Hanna Templeton, his daughter." There, she'd blurted it out. She felt the butterflies in her stomach subside somewhat, and an excitement replaced it. "Is he?" she repeated.

"Oh, Ms. Hanna, I never..." the woman said faintly and preoccupied. "One moment, please."

The woman called her manager to decide how to treat the call, and the doctor in charge was elected to speak with Hanna. When he finally took the call, Hanna was anxious and afraid that perhaps there was a problem. "Miss Templeton?"

His voice was soft, and Hanna softened to its tone. "Yes. Who are you? Do you know where Jay Templeton is?"

"Yes, he is here with us and has been for many years. You say you are his daughter? Where are you?"

"I am studying in England," Hanna explained. "I am an anthropology and theology student in London, and I am digging into my own background, of which I know little. I was hoping to come to the States soon and wondered if I could meet him."

"Hanna, your father is doing well. He is fully rehabilitated, and I'm sure he will be overjoyed to meet you. He speaks of you often." The doctor's voice was hypnotizing.

Hanna heard his words but felt them all the more in her heart. His tone felt so comforting. Hanna felt a deep connection with this voice.

"Ms. Templeton, may I call you Hanna?"

"Yes, of course. Will you be there if I come? Are you his doctor?"

"I am one of his doctors, and of course, I would be honored to meet you."

"Okay. Dr....?"

"My name is Patrick Murphy."

The name sounded familiar to her; the sound of it made her break out in a sweat. She began to smile uncontrollably and said, "Okay, Dr.

Murphy, I will see you in a couple of weeks. I will call when I get back to the States. Will you tell him?" she asked.

"Why don't you send him a letter, Hanna? He would like that."

All Hanna could think of was the letter she had written to Margaret when she was there. "Do I have to? Can't you just tell him? We'll catch up in person... okay?"

Patrick consented, and they agreed to speak in a few weeks. Hanna lingered near the phone for a while, dreaming of that place and feeling edgy about going; yet the thought of meeting this doctor gave her feelings she'd never felt before. Her heart felt so full she could cry.

When Patrick Murphy approached Jay to tell him about Hanna's call, a few days had already passed. He had needed time to consider his approach. Jay was rehabilitated, but that didn't mean he wasn't human. This news would have a great impact. Patrick pondered it for a few days. Eventually, he elected to give it to Jay in the form of a telephone message. He wanted to treat this event with integrity and as an everyday occurrence, so that Jay would feel he was trusted as an adult with this information. It would provide a degree of privacy for him.

And so, on that autumn day, as Jay sat in front of a large picture window in the art studio of the facility, he had multicolored tree leaf transitions before him. Patrick presented him with his message and turned to go.

"Don't go. It's not every day I get a telephone message, doctor; please stay." Jay opened the preprinted form, which was folded in two. It had been years since he'd handled a telephone message, although it felt familiar from memories of his law firm, when a fat wad of messages was stuffed into his hand by his secretary as he whizzed in and out at lightning speed. A message.

He stared at the print, which did not come into focus immediately. The name Hanna was the first word he saw, and he dropped the paper in shock. He looked up, staring at Patrick, his dropped jaw almost drooling. Patrick picked up the message and handed it to him again. Jay tried his best to read every word of the message, and then he read them again.

Patrick sat patiently as Jay processed it. He could see a range of emotions flowing through Jay. His facial expressions, together with his fidgeting, indicated that Jay would need some time before Hanna actually showed up.

Jay's head was down facing the piece of paper, which was beginning to look tattered; Jay's handling and what appeared to be tears had wrangled it. He would read the words, "Your daughter Hanna called, she will call again." That was all it said. His heart felt like it was tearing to bits, while moments of deep joy intervened with his guilt. He cried for days and would not pick up the paintbrush.

Patrick was beginning to wonder if it had been a bad idea, giving him the message. Perhaps the shock of just speaking to her would pull him back from his anguish. He had her telephone number, and decided to use it.

Hanna was in the midst of packing for her trip Stateside when the telephone rang. She felt a tingle all over when she heard it ring. *Hmmm, wonder who that could be*, she thought, and answered the phone with intrigue and excitement. "Hello? Who is this please?" Then she heard Dr. Murphy's voice, and she knew why she'd felt the tingles. She was still thinking more about him than she thought about her dad in recent weeks. "Yes, Patrick, how are you? How nice to hear from you!" she said.

"Hanna, your father seems to have regressed with the news of you. I think he should speak to you on the telephone. It may relieve some of the anxiety he is experiencing. I wonder if you could find it in your heart to have a conversation with him on the telephone."

Hanna hesitated and thought about his question in silence. She closed her eyes for a second, and Nano starred at her intensely. His eyes were like huge pools of the unknown, and as she looked into them, she saw images of her father from childhood. He was smiling and laughing, and she did not feel any darkness coming from him. Nano nudged her with his nose; he looked up at the stars, and Hanna's intent followed. He showed her a picture of Jay standing next to one of his paintings. It was magnificent, an image of their house and the garden on the side. It felt like home, and she had no hard feelings. Hanna could only feel joy inside. She whispered in Nano's ear, "I will speak with my dad; protect me." Nano nodded to her, and she knew he would.

"Sure, Patrick, put him on the line. I would love to speak with him!"

Patrick was surprised at her response and asked her to hold. He found Jay in the day room staring out the window. Conveniently, they had him in a wheelchair, and Patrick was able to wheel him to the telephone. He said nothing on the way, and when they reached his office, he put on the brake and closed his door. He handed Patrick the phone and said, "Hanna's on the phone for you, Jay."

Jay lifted his hand weakly, and Patrick gently put the phone in his hand. He held onto his hand as Jay took the phone to his ear. Patrick watched Jay's eyes as he listened to Hanna speak…

"Hello? Dad, is that you? It's me, Hanna! Betya thought you'd never hear from me again, eh? Me too! I never thought I'd contact you either. But I have good reason."

Hanna listened for a response and got silence.

"Hello?" she said rather loudly. "Heeellooo."

"Yeah, yeah, I'm here, Hanny, yeah, I'm here. Give me a minute to listen to you. Give me a minute, okay?"

Hanna heard his voice. She stopped short too. It ripped all the way through her. His voice had not changed a bit. And she still feared it. She wanted to count suddenly; she wanted to grab onto solid objects so as not to get pulled off. Her fear could take her far away, and she sought solace in a crystal that sat beside her. She grabbed it and held it to her heart; it provided her with a brilliant ray of light, which she dipped in and out of, regaining stature with each dose.

"Hi, Dad. I'm in school in England. How are you?"

"I'm a painter now," he said. "But I haven't painted since you called. Thank you for calling back."

"I didn't call, Dad. Your doctor called me; he was concerned. He told me that you have become a painter. I look forward to seeing your art."

"Thank you, Hanny. When are you coming?"

"Would two weeks work for you? Can you fit me into your schedule?" Hanna teased him, and he laughed.

"Yes, I think I could fit you in!"

"Okay, I will call you as soon as I know which day, Dad. You stay good now, and paint. Will you paint one for me?"

"What a great idea! Indeed, I will, Hanna."

"Well then, bye for now," Hanna said.

Hanna couldn't stop thinking about Patrick, the doctor. She was surprised she wasn't more interested in her dad, but she felt her motivation swayed by her attraction to this man. *Could he be the one?* she wondered. She missed Margaret so at times like this. She yearned to share these things but knew in her heart that she had to wait and that Margaret was benefiting without her somehow.

She knew they would see each other during her visit, a brief interlude for some reason being allowed by the wolves and Trudy. In fact, Trudy was encouraging this visit, and Hanna wondered a bit about that. She wondered how restricted her time with Margaret would be. After all, they were both twenty-five already, and the transition from guardian to adult friend and companion was happening. She knew it didn't matter, though; she would always consider Trudy her mother and teacher and friend. She trusted her with all of her heart and never thought to question her wishes. That's just the way it had always been.

When finally Hanna arrived in the States and settled in at the stone cottage at the corner of the street that sometimes disappeared from ordinary sight, the three resumed the peaceful trust among them; their days and nights were consumed with reintroductions to and spontaneous chatter about mortality and life as we know it and as we dream it.

It was during those shortened autumn days among the changing colors and the chill in the air that Dr. Murphy decided to visit Hanna before she went to the hospital. He, too, felt some connection with her and a deepening urge to meet her. When he came up the front path, they all saw him.

Hanna knew who he was immediately and jumped to the front door. She practically fell out onto the front path and ran toward him. At about two feet, she stopped short, and her hands waved back to steady herself, her hair blown all in her face. She looked up in between the strands to see the most handsome man she'd ever set her eyes on. Her mouth opened slightly as she stared.

He said, "Careful now; don't let a bug fly in," and gently touched the top of her lip, brushing her hair to the side.

Hanna closed her mouth abruptly and jumped at his touch. She looked at him scornfully for a split second, but the very sight of him brought her such joy, she was smiling again in no time. "Come and sit down, Patrick. Would you like some tea perhaps?"

Trudy came in from the bedroom and greeted him with a handshake and nod of her head. "So, you are the doctor I keep hearing about. I am Trudy Goodenough, these girls' guardian. I see that you are my girl's father's guardian. How are things?"

Patrick shook Trudy's hand and sat next to her. "Jay has transformed, ma'am. I hope you will accompany Hanna when she visits. You will find a different person, I believe."

"Ah, Jay was quite a victim of his time, doctor. I am glad that he was able to move away from that," Trudy said.

"What are you talking about?" Hanna interjected.

Patrick touched Hanna's hand gently and said endearingly, "Your father has transformed, Hanna. His voice has not changed, but his words have; his intent has. Are you able to separate the two?"

"It is a big lesson for me in forgiveness. I can, Patrick, and I feel comfortable with your guidance too."

"Why don't you come over with me now? Jay is having a very good day, and he finished your painting."

Hanna looked over at Trudy to see what she thought. She looked to Margaret too.

"Hanna, you should go now. It's spontaneous, and you won't have to wait anymore. Go on!" Margaret piped up. She moved over to a chair close to Hanna and put her arm over her shoulder, leaning forward and resting her chin on the back of the chair. "You'll go, right?" she whispered in her ear.

"Only if you all go with me."

Margaret sat straight up and loosened her hold on Hanna. "You won't catch me anywhere near that place!"

Nala also reared up on her hind legs and fell over on top of Margaret, pushing her off balance slightly. She held onto the back of her chair.

"Okay, Mar, I understand," Hanna said, calming her. "But Trudy, you'll come, won't you?"

"Hanna, I think Dr. Murphy will make an excellent escort for you; you'll have time to chat without us," Trudy said and smiled warmly, looking at them both as one in her imagination. Their spirits merged impeccably; she saw no explosions or reactions, only sheer integration of energy between the two.

Yet Hanna felt fireworks in her belly every time she glanced at him or heard his voice; the thought of being alone with him caused a hurricane inside of her. She wasn't sure how to feel, and this scared her; she wasn't used to being unsure. At uni in London, she was a star student. Her projects on digs and her abilities to find rare things and instinctively know what they were and where they came from had provided her with a high reputation, and Hanna was enjoying it. The long hard days she had spent with Trudy where she would spend an entire day talking to a rock or a plant or a root were paying off.

Hanna had learned the art of communication with any object, and it was serving her well in her studies. But now, all of her skills and tools would not come to her aid; she was in unknown territory and treading lightly. Affairs of her heart and her soul were in play, and she was walking into both of them head-first with open heart, though her baseline was trepidation.

"Okay, Patrick, I'll just go change, and we can go."

Patrick smiled and leaned back in his chair with relief; he and Trudy exchanged sighs and a chuckle while Hanna was out of the room.

"Seems you've taken a fancy to our Hanna?" Trudy kicked his foot playfully and laughed.

"She's totally besotted!" Margaret added and laughed out loud.

Patrick blushed and looked down as he played with his fingers and tapped his right foot slightly. "I'm just here to help, as I said," Patrick said quietly.

Trudy turned and looked at him directly. "Don't lead my girl on now, doctor. If you have no intentions with her, do tell me now—or maybe you are just being modest?"

Patrick shifted in his chair. He rubbed his nose back and forth, staring at Trudy. "Well, she is a lovely lady, and a smart one too! I assume she'll go back to London and probably earn a doctorate." He stopped for a moment and looked at Trudy, feeling very awkward. "I don't believe Hanna is the marrying type."

Trudy stood up and slapped her thigh. She hooted out loud, and Margaret giggled to herself, curling up in her chair.

Patrick stared at the two of them, confused and perplexed. His nose was beginning to turn red with all his rubbing.

Hanna emerged from the bedroom dressed in a peasant skirt and blouse, a flowery pattern in orange, yellow, and brown hues; she blended well with the autumn leaves outside. She knew that her color combination would reflect blending, which was clearly her intent. She smiled at Patrick, who was gawking at her, and said, "Okay, let's go. You know, I haven't even told you why I wanted to meet him…" Her words slowed as she took his arm and waved at Trudy and Margaret nonchalantly as they headed for the door.

Mar and Trudy sat astonished, speechless at Hanna's manner, and Patrick just followed her.

By the time they reached the hospital, which was about an hour outside of town, Hanna had had enough time to tell Patrick her whole life story and the reason for her visit with Jay. "So, Patrick, do you think he will remember anything about our ancestors? I need to check out all of my dreams and see where it's all coming from. Like I said, I'm doing a school project, but also, it's the dreams I have; I'm sure they are about our ancestors, and I have to verify something with him."

"Yes, Hanna, I understand," Patrick agreed. "I do believe Jay is aware of his past, although we have never discussed it. I should be interested in hearing about this as well."

They parked and walked toward the entrance. Hanna was preoccupied with Patrick but still felt a deep anxiety tug her gut as they approached the building. She almost felt inclined to count as she looked up ahead at the entrance.

Patrick noticed her change in color, her face paling, and her walk weakening. He put a hand on her shoulder, and she looked him in the eyes. She moved toward him with her whole body and leaned it slightly on his side. Like her wolf, she tried to circle him, and his arm caught her halfway around and pulled her to him tight. Her head tilted back so as not to knock straight into his jaw, and they smiled and laughed lightly as they walked into the hospital's lobby.

"Why don't you sit here, and I'll go and get Jay," Patrick said. "It's such a nice day!"

"I want to see his paintings, Patrick. Can I come to his studio?"

"Oh yes, I completely forget. Of course, you'll want to see the painting he just finished for you. Yes, why don't you wait here anyway? I'll come and get you."

Hanna sat down and wondered why she had to wait behind. She felt abandoned there and tried to collect herself. She closed her eyes, and Nano was jumping and howling and squealing; she heard him saying, "It's nothing, Hanna, it's nothing. Have an amazing experience here with your dad, and perhaps a love? This fear you have serves you not and warns you of only what your *mind* creates. Leave your mind for today, for this afternoon, and enjoy it with your heart and your soul. Enjoy now the forgiveness that you have become. This is the gift of forgiveness! Today will bring you all that you ask for, my dear one. Take it all in, as I will too. I thank you for this journey, young Hanna!" he said and disappeared into space.

Hanna opened her eyes, and her dad stood three feet in front of her. She jumped but didn't have much room, so she sat back down. She looked up. He towered over her, and he was smiling brightly. His eyes were alive and playful. He had aged, she noticed, no balding, but his hair was white and stood up straight above his head, Mohican style, gelled tight into form. He was wearing a casual-looking uniform, khakis and shirt, and he wore slippers on his feet. She questioned that and thought it was probably due to his inpatient status at the hospital.

"Hello there, my daughter," Jay said and waited for her to respond.

"Hi, Dad," she said shortly, like it was just yesterday he was checking her homework. Like he was just going to say, "Hello, princess, had a good day at school?" Like he did once in a while then.

"Hanna, would you like to see the painting I made for you?"

"Yes, that would be nice, thank you."

Patrick took Hanna's hand, and she followed him as Jay led them to his studio. It was a grand room, one of those wonderful creations of Victorian architecture, a round room; the hospital had provided this space to him, and all of the patients enjoyed the art. It had a circular vault ceiling, which climbed a couple of stories; the top was formed with round windows, allowing light to stream into the room from all directions.

"Here's your painting, Hanna." Jay was standing in front of a three-by-one-and-a-half-foot canvas on which he had created their home.

Hanna gazed at it surprised to see the resemblance and how much she remembered and he had remembered. Her first comment was, as she pointed to the stoop of the porch, "Mom's shoes are missing."

Jay grabbed a paintbrush and immediately began sketching in her shoes; somehow magically his lines blended into the painting as if they had always been there. "What else, my child? What else is missing? Help me out here," he said.

She winced when she heard him say, "my child," and studied the image, sensing the feelings of home she felt in her belly. "There, over here," she said, pointing. "Wasn't there always a wheelbarrow with flowers in it? And what about Ma's clothesline?"

Jay jumped around grabbing tubes of paint, mixing them up, making random marks on the canvas that continued to become part of the painting.

Hanna watched, amazed at what she was seeing.

Patrick stayed in the background, witnessing the miracle. He felt very warm inside and wasn't sure himself what he was experiencing, but he knew it was sacred, that it came from God, and he knew to be quiet and watch.

Both wolves had accompanied Hanna. They wanted to be sure it went well, and more so, they yearned for this merging. Their own journeys required it. It was an exercise in total forgiveness, total gratitude. They felt sacred humbleness to see their sister walking her path with forgiveness for the atrocities she had endured. She knew she would never be who she was today had her dad not killed them all. It was a thought that came in and out of her; guilt tried to catch it by its tail and keep it close, but she released it well. Hanna knew better; gratitude embraced her today, and she received it with grace. *Guilt would serve no purpose today*, she thought, and she chased it off by looking again at her home on canvas and directing her dad to include her own memories into it.

Nano and Nala celebrated this day; they held ceremony with their higher ones and brought in the winds and the soft clouds to ride upon.

Their intent was solely to commune, and to be as one. The wolves knew that the girls were growing up and would be choosing their lifetime passions soon. The wolves knew their potential and were ready to guide them on these paths. But today, they witnessed Hanna's journey as theirs; it was a monumental day, one of those days for the rest of life and death.

The feelings Hanna had were not her normal self-assured brain-instigated intents. She couldn't quite translate the urges inside into words. She would try and express verbally, and only grunts and squeals came out. Jay didn't seem to notice as he, too, was communicating without words, only for him it was with the strokes of his paintbrush.

Chapter 10

Margaret studied sound healing after she finished her GED. She was not inclined to book study and decided not to join in the academic life that Hanna had pursued. Instead, she and Trudy searched for a teacher for her, and she began in the local church choir.

She discovered a yoga studio in town and began to learn the ancient art of yoga from a yogi who had come from India to teach. The studio was tucked away downtown in a cheap old warehouse that was decorated with old parachutes lining the walls and ceilings, and the concrete floor was painted a bright yellow, covered with bamboo mats, cushions, and blankets. The acoustics were very good, and during classes, someone would always begin to sing or chant. Margaret loved those moments and always joined in. Her biggest dream was to somehow combine the yoga exercise with music.

Trudy was teaching her about spiritual power centers throughout her body. In yoga class, they called them chakras. With Trudy she learned about each one and its character and its purpose.

"Dear Mar," Trudy would say, "hold your hand just above your belly, and you will feel the energy of your chakras. Close your eyes and visualize a spiral of color within each one. They all have a different color, my child, do you see? Can you hear their tones?"

Mar would sit and try, and the harder she tried, the less she would sense.

Trudy would say, "Mar, remember always, be in your center when you exercise, and you will sense yourself. You cannot do this from your brain. Why don't you go sit outside in the garden for a while and awaken your belly?"

Nala would follow her into the garden; on cold nights they would sit there in the snow, and she would keep Mar warm. It was during those nights that Margaret learned the most about the power of sound and how it healed her. In the dead of night, when freezing fog enveloped the house, she and Nala would sit or dance under the moon. And Margaret would sing. Her tones and the wolf's howls blended like silk and cream into harmonies that Margaret felt in her body and in her power centers. She could feel them unraveling and stretching into the heavens, and she learned to pull them back into her at will. She also learned that each chakra had an animal spirit who would express its voice in her chants. Her tone would change to remind her of the animal spirit living in each chakra.

Trudy was pleased with Mar's progress and encouraged her to go out in the world and teach her findings. "You are a pioneer, Margaret child, woman that you are now. It is time for you to spread your wings too. Leave this nest that you love so dearly. It is time for you to build your own nest."

"Yes, Trudy, as grateful as I am to you and the only real home I have ever known, I too feel in my bones that change is coming. I feel great things inside of me, Trudy, and I don't know how. There is this gigantic hole in my life, and its size is as huge as my dream, though I cannot yet decipher it. I can only feel its size."

"Ahh, Mar, you are indeed walking into a very large time in your life. You have transformed into a magical sound goddess. Hanna won't recognize you! I am very pleased, my daughter. This home will always be your home, and the home you build will become an extension of this. We are so fortunate, you know. Be grateful, child."

"Trudy, I keep having visions of me standing in front of thousands of people. I am seeing it at every turn now, and still have no idea how this will manifest in my life."

"Yes, I see it too. You will find your way," was Trudy's response.

And so it came to pass that Margaret became a sage of sound. She began with small workshops, and within no time, the halls she booked for her events became larger and larger. Her four-hour events became weekend festivals of sound, and it was finally time for Hanna to come home from abroad for one of Margaret's biggest and most prestigious events in New York City. It was to be held in Central Park on summer solstice eve, and the buzz around the event had awakened the upper Manhattan conscience.

Margaret had invited other yogis for the weekend, which was packed with New Age and shamanic teachers, including her most important teacher next to Trudy, Lynn Andrews.

Hanna was so excited as she boarded the plane for New York, she nearly forgot her carry-on luggage, which contained her special gift for Margaret. It was an ancient flute she had found on one of her digs. It had called to her, and somehow she knew it was okay for her to take the item from the collection. She held her bag with care, feeling its vibrations moving in the bag; she sent it a caring thought to calm it and searched for her seat—a window, as she'd requested. As the plane filled, she was grateful that the center seat remained vacant.

She knew that Nano would be flying with her this night. She set her head back onto her neck cushion and closed her eyes. Color filled her vision as her spirit jetted out to meet Nano. He was solemn, and Hanna felt he had something to say. She put her ear to his breath as he gave her a vision of a cougar; she was on the hunt and stared at Hanna like prey. Hanna backed into Nano as she watched this massively graceful creature step forward toward them, staring her in the eye still, leaving Hanna mesmerized in her gaze.

Nano pawed at Hanna, causing her to turn. He scowled at her and growled, "Don't let her take you, Hanna. She is stalking Margaret. You will see."

"What?" Hanna reacted and fell out of balance, awaking abruptly on the airplane.

The steward was passing out drinks as she opened her eyes, and Hanna realized she had stretched out on all three seats. She wondered where the passenger in the aisle seat had gone and sat up to look. "Tea, coffee? Soft drink?" the woman asked. Her prim uniform and cap looked official, and Hanna looked up attentively.

"Um, can I just have some water please? Is there any food?" she asked, feeling a need to ground.

"Food will be served shortly," the stewardess said curtly in her cute British accent.

Hanna smiled at her sweetly and took her water.

She drifted back to her dream, and found the cougar still staring at her.

She heard Nano growl again. "Send her away, Hanna; she serves no purpose here."

She asked him, "What does she want?"

"Why don't you ask her?"

Hanna stared the black cougar down, and she fell from her feet and rolled onto her back, submitting. "Why are you here?" Hanna asked.

The cougar turned and leaped to the air straight from her belly and darted in and out of Hanna's vision. It made her feel uncomfortable as she stirred the winds and caused a storm.

"Who are you, and what do you want?" Hanna screamed inside. She felt herself weakening by the moment.

The cougar screeched back at her scream; it was owllike almost, and then she lunged toward Hanna, only to halt in front of her. Their energies collided, and Hanna fell over.

She woke up in her seat on the plane again. This time there was the smell of hot food in the air, and she decided to stay "awake" for a while and eat.

As she sat, she wondered about her dream and the cougar and who she was. Her wolf had not provided her with an answer, and neither had the cougar except for one thing that kept niggling her. The cougar caused chaos. This thought kept coming up. Her energy was chaotic, she acted crazy-like, and there was nothing calm about her. Even when she hypnotized her at the beginning, Hanna had experienced being "dislodged" from herself. This animal was plain outright awkward. And still, why was she dreaming about her?

Now that Hanna had left the dreamtime, Nano set to work. He put his nose to the ground and began sniffing out the cougar and found her deep beneath the earth. She was not a normal cougar who lives in the forest, but an underling shadow-being who took the form of a cougar to fool anyone it met. Nano sat with the shadowy being and nudged into some kind of communication, although it was almost unreachable. Nano knew that this being would wreak havoc in the girls' lives if he didn't transform it somehow. He was still discovering whom it was attached to. Was this one of Nala's discarded shadows, left behind and forgotten? And why was Hanna being approached to pick it up?

Hanna was mopping up the gravy around the tiny ounce of chicken in her compact airplane meal. The plane was experiencing turbulent winds, and everything shook on her tray as they passed through them. It was the same feeling as the cougar caused, and she drifted back again to its image. She heard Nano say to her, "Don't focus on her; she is here to disturb you. She is a shadow-being that belonged to Nala and Margaret, who gave it up in recent years. She has come back to cause chaos at Margaret's event. We must not let her."

Hanna couldn't believe it. She was astonished and finished her meal as quickly as she could so she could resume her dreaming. The onboard movie was about to start, but she had a more important movie to be in. She could feel Nano calling her in her belly, and as soon as she could give her food tray back and lie back under the thin blanket, she joined him and found that he had company. He sat among what seemed like a hundred animals. They were all deep in a trance, and she stepped in silently and sat down next to her wolf. She saw that Nala and Trudy and her elk were there as well, but she did not feel Margaret's presence.

Nano hushed her, and she was reminded that her thoughts were as loud as day on this dreaming plane. "Leave your questions at the gateway," he sent her. "Stay in witness, child."

Hanna quieted herself and opened herself to what was about to occur. She noticed that all of the animals were slowly rising and walking to a central point. Nano stayed with Hanna and made her stay where she was. The animals were all beasts of prey, the carnivorous ones. She noted the eagle and the lions and tigers and wolves. The cougar was prowling among them all, but none would bat an eyelid at it. When it approached one, it would stick its snout in the air and turn its back on it. The cougar would do a little gig each time it touched one. She seemed to take pleasure at their distaste for her.

Farther afield, Hanna could see other kinds of the animal kingdom. The grazers were on the foothills; she could see the deer the elk, the elephants, and the buffalo; winged ones above sang a chorus of tones, which she knew was orchestrating the animals below.

Nano nudged her, and she looked over toward the water in the distance. There was a dark cloud levitating above the water and on the horizon; it clouded and bore a shadow that did not make sense, as the light was not reflecting there. Nano looked at her intensely.

"What do you want me to do?" she asked impatiently. "Yeah, I can see it is shadow. It's not real, Nano. You don't have to give it your attention if you don't need it, you know," she said boldly to him.

Nano walked up close to her and landed a slobbery lick on her cheek. She had clearly passed the test. But would Margaret? Hanna couldn't help wondering what might occur if this cougar showed up at her presentation.

Nano hushed her again. Then he did something she could not have ever expected. He growled at her and banished her from the dream.

Hanna woke up with a start. She had forgotten she was on the airplane and couldn't understand why she was crying. It had been years since she'd cried. As a comfort, she thought about Patrick and hoped he would be at the airport to pick her up. Their long-distance romance had endured over five years, and she hoped that during this visit, they might find a way to be together more. Her heart filled twice over, and she quickly forgot about the cougar while she imagined herself in Patrick's arms. Fortunately, he was able to visit every few months in London; he had also gone with her on digs in Egypt and England. A very resourceful man, he took a great interest in Hanna's work and was delighted with her insight. Their relationship kept her close to Jay too, and Patrick would give her reports on him. Only a couple more hours, and she'd be in his arms.

Nano traveled quickly across the seas; he was in a hurry to reach his Nala before the cougar did. He remembered that part of her well—the time when she had disposed of this shadow. She had sent her to the ocean deep for cleansing, and she told her to come back in a balanced way. This shadow was a shadow and knew not balance, and Nano had seen her root to the ocean shadows. He knew he could not stop what was about to occur, but he hoped to soften it at least. He wanted Nala to be prepared at least.

Nala was unaware. Basking in Margaret's recovery and success, she was unwary too. Her animal instinct had become lazy within Margaret's protective tones and connections with spirit. She'd become lazy. And the shadows had begun to taunt her well before the cougar made her appearance; Nala had been feeling lazy and hazy. She didn't care too much about anything, and Margaret was beginning to feel her weight. It was heavy and lifeless. She'd been waiting for Hanna's arrival and hoped Nano might be able to help.

The two women were strangers to look at; they'd each developed her own style. Now thirty years old, they embraced warmly and silently at Kennedy Airport.

Patrick stood aside, as their reunion was so deep. Trudy stood with him and tapped him on the shoulder. "They are sisters, Patrick, dear, dear sisters."

He smiled and said, "I understand, Trudy. Hanna and I will have our time; I'm in no hurry. Let them reacquaint. I've seen Hanna many times in the past years."

As the two walked hand in hand to baggage claim, Hanna took hold of Mar's arm suddenly and tugged. "Mar, I had the weirdest dreams on the way over. Did you?"

"Well, I've been feeling very nervous, and I don't normally. Like suddenly I have doubts…"

"Mar, let all the doubts wash away with the sands." Hanna waved her hands over Mar's head and faced her for a moment, standing in the middle of the baggage claim. "I clear all doubt from you, and if any shadows find a place with you, I send them off!" Hanna proclaimed, and then said quietly, "There, that will take care of her!"

"Who?" Margaret asked.

"I told you, Mar, from my dream. It's sticking to me, and I don't want a speck of it near you!"

Patrick caught up with the two as they waited for Hanna's bag to come out. Hanna ran to him, and they embraced inconsolably. Hanna kept raising her leg in an attempt to ride Patrick, while he dodged her but was equally aroused. Their expressions back and forth were not understood nor needed to be. Patrick was a strong tall man; his arms and arched back created a cave that Hanna fit into impeccably. She closed her eyes, and her heart was full; tears came, and she wiped her eyes on his sleeve. He felt her back contract and release in his hold, and he let her cry.

Trudy came over to Hanna and put her hand on the back of her head. She felt it immediately, and her comfort gave her a place to put her tears. She lifted her head in joy, with her bright smile shining on Trudy. Trudy's eyes were wet, too, as they reunited in the middle of the baggage hall.

"Margaret, please tell me where we are going and what you are presenting. Is it today, or do we have a few days for some time together?" Hanna continued, "Hey, Mar, since we are in New York, we have to go to the theater, see a concert, eh?"

"Hanna, this is a dream come true, to present this talk here in New York, and for you to be here with me! I can't believe my good fortune! Oh, I almost forgot. There's someone there I'd like you to meet."

Hanna interrupted her, "Someone? Do tell!"

Mar looked around and didn't really want to share her "girl talk" with Patrick. "I will. It's girl talk, though."

Patrick laughed aloud. "Ah, Margaret, but I want to know too!"

Trudy piped up, "Yes, Mar, who are you talking about?"

"Well, we only met a couple of days ago… and it's still hard to describe. I'm going to wait. You will all meet her soon."

Hanna, Patrick, and Trudy all thought in unison, *Did she say "her"?* Their glances in sync looked up at Mar, who was looking intensely into her lap at her fingernails. She could feel them staring at her. She knew there was no problem—they were just surprised—yet she could not lift her head to them. She thought of "her." This woman had appeared out of nowhere a couple of days before. There was darkness about her that Mar was attracted to, yet she knew it was not healthy for her. She wondered whether she should have said anything in the first place.

Nala had not noticed anything; she was lounging. Margaret knew she needed to consult with Nano and had waited for Hanna's arrival. There were brief moments while Trudy, Hanna and Patrick had waited for her to respond. Margaret felt herself falling out of time, she was connecting with Nano.

"She feels like she is the answer to my dreams, yet she frightens me so, I don't know!" She said to Trudy, Hanna and Patrick.

Nano was realizing very quickly that they were dealing with the same shadow-being who had been stalking Hanna's dreams. He hadn't made it in time, and Mar had already befriended her. This would make things complicated. He was grateful, however, that Mar had approached him about her; now he had a chance, and he also would need to give Nala a shaking when he found her.

He was intent on reaching her before they arrived at the exhibition hall where Margaret's presentation was going to begin that evening. The car was stuffy for him, but he persevered, and eventually Margaret gave him her attention. "This woman you have met, tell me about her."

Nano sensed the woman. Margaret imagined in her mind and could feel a strange sensation in her heart. It didn't feel comfortable. Nano caught her vision and stepped into it promptly. He saw the shadow-being and saw through her immediately. He also noted that she looked zombielike. He asked Margaret, "Does she usually look like that?"

Margaret noted to him, "No, Nano, she's different now. Yesterday, she was very beautiful and seducing; she even bought me a new dress to wear tonight!"

"Today you see her with your third eye, your soul, Mar; you see through her. She is that shadow-being of Nala. We must find Nala!"

Margaret lamented and laughed slightly… "Nala has turned into a lazy old dog who lies in front of the fire all day. She has not communicated with me since I started teaching a couple of years ago. I wanted to ask you about that."

Nano pushed her on the side of her head with his nose. "Why did you not tell Trudy? Dear young woman, you are in great danger! How could you allow your spirit wolf to languish so?"

"I thought she was supposed to take care of me," Mar said. "Nobody told me I needed to look after her!"

Nano pawed her shoulder, and she fell into Hanna in the backseat of the car.

"You okay?" Hanna asked.

Margaret looked at her vacantly; she was dreaming and could not respond.

Margaret said to both Nano in the dream and Hanna in the car, "Someone's going to have to help me find Nala! I have a show tonight. What should I do—cancel it?"

Trudy interjected, "You certainly will not, my daughter. This will be a good test for you."

"A test? A test, you say?" Mar shouted. "Haven't I been tested enough? Trudy, you know where I have been and how far I have come. Won't you help me out here?"

"You should not have let your Nala go so. Now you must find her," Trudy said stubbornly.

"Trudy, I have a show tonight!"

"Yes, I know."

"Child, listen to me," Nano stated. "I want you to think about the last time you saw her. Think clearly and tell me everything you see. Take me to when you separated; think carefully of the last sight you had of her as she went on her way. I will follow her from that point, my dear. I cannot guarantee that tonight will be without an incident. Life awaits you, dear one."

Nano disappeared from the car as he pursued Mar's stalker; everyone was feeling tense. Patrick tried to relax them by asking Mar to sing for them. Hanna had not yet heard Mar's angelic voice. Margaret complied and sang an old Native American song she loved. Hanna began drumming on her suitcase, and Trudy chanted.

In a deep creviced tunnel, far down in the ocean, the eellike creature existed. She was once a spirit, but it was long ago when she splintered off. She liked to resent and create confusion around her. She thrived once on the power to make another miserable, and she had implanted herself within Margaret as a child after the fire. Margaret threw her out and left her nowhere to go. She thrived without Margaret, and now she was back to claim what was hers. Her body quivered and sent off electric shocks around her, causing the water in her tunnel to suck her out into the massive sea. Instinctively, she swam up and reached the surface; once up there, she knew she would find Margaret. Her encounters with her allies had served her well, and her cougar certainly would know what to do now. Her mission was to reenter Margaret, to bring her down, back to where she belonged. This creature had no idea what she was up against!

By the time they had checked into the hotel and washed up, it was time to go to dinner and then over to the exhibition hall at Central Park.

Margaret's seminar began at 8:00 p.m. It would be the most exciting night of her life! They wanted to get good New York Italian pasta in them and some hearty red wine for her vocal cords.

The restaurant was busy and noisy; the aroma of tomato sauce and steamed clams filled the dining room. They even all ate dessert. Margaret, enjoying her port and lemon, swished it around as she cleansed her throat chakra. She had one more hour, and it was time for her to begin her process.

She left everyone behind as she headed over to prepare for her presentation. As she walked, she began to chant inside, working from her root chakra up to her crown, cleansing, clearing, and chanting love into her heart and down to her root. It was an exercise that had become second nature to her, and she performed with no thought. Her thoughts were on her clothing, the stage, whether they had set everything up right, whether the music would work, and whether anyone would show up.

She always wondered, even though her presentations only grew in size. Her thoughts always betrayed her heart. *Why is that?* she wondered, and knew that it was time to stop "thinking." She drew in a breath and concentrated on her third and fourth chakras, her shaman and heart centers. Those would be her tools tonight. She was up for the tests Nano had cautioned her of and was clearly looking forward to bringing Nala back to life; she also knew that this woman was a metaphor of her relationship with Nala—zombielike.

"Great spirit," she prayed, "I ask for guidance, love, and protection tonight. Help me stay in my center tonight." As she entered the hall and headed to her area, she continued her prayer: "Great spirit, awaken my Nala, awaken her now. Bring her to me and let her accompany me this night on stage." She prayed to the stars above and to mother earth below. She called in all of her allies, her sage and her drum, her visions of essence, of God; she brought all of them in to her centers, her heart, and her intuition. And as she walked, she could *see* a long trail of squirrels, chipmunks, and rabbits following behind her, and in the background the sound of a flute echoed the bird caws and calls. She continued, "Great spirit, I am grateful. I forgive my Nala for getting lazy, and I invite her back; let me hear her howls with my song, my wolf song. I sing, *aho!*"

As Margaret walked among the long rows of stalls, all full of teachings of the unknown, she could feel the diversity of spirit around her; she could feel the merging of this diversity under one roof, and she felt deep respect for what she was about to impart on this general public. All of her relations would be in the audience tonight—so special—and she hoped that Nala would be joining too.

The curtained-off area where the presentation was to be held was closed still, and Margaret slipped in between the beige-colored hangings and walked up to the head of the room, where she would be presenting. There was a table and chair as she'd requested and a microphone and a small amp ready for use. She sat down with her bag and began to pull out all of the sacred items she had chosen for her altar. She took her time setting it up, smoothing out the warm, soft wolf skin she had acquired, and spreading an altar cloth over it. She honored the four directions with her personal power crystals and then scattered sage and copal over it. She lit a tiny twig of sage and let it burn in her cherished abalone shell. Margaret set a small candle next to each crystal holding the powers of the four directions, and she blew onto them gently to conjure up the aromas and the spirits of her altar. She washed her face and head in the sage smoke, breathing gently and feeling the filter of the sage cleanse her breath and spirit.

Margaret was startled by the sound of the partition moving and a voice that sounded familiar yet she couldn't identify it. She looked up to see a delicious blond woman, dressed in flowing skirt and blouse the colors of tropical cocktails. All she needed was a cherry on her hat and some whipped cream, and Margaret would have eaten her like an ice-cream cone. Mar stared at her as she walked up with no hesitation, with a bright red lipsticked smile and her arms outstretched for a hug.

"You must be Margaret; so good to meet you. I'm Lynn."

Margaret nearly jumped out of her seat. "Lynn Andrews?" she guessed.

"Yes, dear one, I am looking forward to hearing you tonight."

"You are looking forward to seeing me? But you are my guide and inspiration, Lynn! Your books and the teachings of the Sisterhood of the Shields have accompanied and sometimes led all of my training! I walk this path with so much joy and gratitude to you; it is I who await your talk, Ms. Andrews."

Lynn became serious and looked at her intently.

"Margaret, you are about to have an extraordinary experience tonight. You are walking into it so innocently, yet I know you are aware; your gratitude keeps you strong, young one. We are here to protect and honor *you*, and we will be here *for you* tonight." She looked at Margaret with deep concern, and Mar opened her mouth to protest. Lynn put her finger to her lips. She shut her eyes for a moment, and when Margaret looked deep into them, she saw a black wolf with piercing blue eyes. Nala materialized in Lynn's eyes, and Mar could see her finally getting up from her bed next to the fire. Margaret felt Nala focusing on Lynn, who smiled and said, "Yes, Mar, you watch that wolf of yours!" She laughed, gave Margaret a kiss on her forehead, and slipped out of the conference area.

As Lynn left, Trudy, Hanna, and Patrick arrived. Margaret called them in to reserve their seats.

They all gathered around the altar. Trudy began a prayer, and they ended it with toning of their heart chakras, letting out long-winded vowel-sounding tones of "Ahhhhhhh." At one point, Margaret sensed the harmonic produced by their voices and released it to the room, where people were already coming in and sitting down in the three hundred or so chairs facing the stage.

As they took their seats, Lynn sat with them, and at each end, they left one seat vacant for the wolves. Nano sat next to Hanna, and the seat next to Lynn remained vacant. Margaret wondered if Nala would make it or not.

The present became infused with tsunami strength as Margaret felt herself walk to the podium, reach for the microphone, and take her seat in front of her altar. She lit each candle in silence as the crowd watched and the tones of Jonathan Goldman sounded in the background. He was playing a xylophone; the deep sounds penetrated into the crowd as Margaret opened her mouth to speak.

"Good evening, kindred spirits!" Margaret greeted the crowd. She let out a heart chakra tone, "*Ahhhhhhhhh*. Can I hear you all sing, *Ahhhhhhhhh*?" The area hummed in the key of F, and even the canvas partitions rippled from the vibrations.

"Did you hear that, everyone? Did you see that on the boundaries of our space here? Sound can move things. Sound can heal. Sound will change your point of view. When we work with sound from within our bodies, we can touch any dis-ease from within. Depending on your trust and skill, sound can be the instrument for anything you do in this world. It's important to know the anatomy of sound so that you can connect with every aspect of it—the rhythm, the key, the note, the vibrations it causes… Close your eyes for a moment, everyone. *ImagIne* your favorite tone; hear it from all around you in stereo twice over. Listen to the beat of the syllables of the words; hear each note as a beat, or skip one and create another rhythm.

"The use of sound is infinite; I am only touching the first gateways. Let's practice for a moment, everyone." Margaret walked over to her flip board, which had a diagram of a human body and the seven chakras beautifully illustrated in rainbow colors up the body from the butt to the top of the head. As she reviewed each chakra with the crowd, she had them tone the sacred vowel sound for each energy center. She discussed the movement of the energy within each center and how it needed to be cleansed regularly.

Margaret looked down into the audience between sentences and saw her family—Trudy, Hanna, and Patrick. She saw Lynn and the seat, still vacant, next to her. She tried to ignore the pain in her heart and filled it with light. She could not let this bother her now.

Nano and Nala were on the roof of the exhibition hall. He had managed to beckon her this far, but she would not go into the hall. "Okay, sister, it is time to release and begin again. You have sat in Margaret's glory for too long, and your light is weak. Your shadow-being is stalking you, and it is up to you if you will let her kill you or not."

Nano got up on his hind legs and howled up at the stars; he landed with his front paws on top of Nala, digging straight into her ribs. Nala jumped up and snarled; her curled-up nose pointed straight down at Nano's neck, and she threatened him with a glare that stabbed in his heart. Her shrill screech into the night could be heard in the hall below, and Margaret began to sweat at the sound of it. Her stomach was churning, and she wanted to vomit.

Nala sneered at him. "Yeah, you think you're so sacred, all close with your human and spreading all that love. Yeah, you ignore the darkness and my pain. You never knew who I was; you never wanted to know who I was. You just discarded what didn't serve the girl. You just tossed a whole side of me to the sharks."

Nano knew by now that the shadow-being had reached Nala and engulfed her with resentment and hate. He knew his only weapon was love. The question was when to inject it. Would she receive it, and what if she rejected it?

Nala was not finished. "You think you are so smooth, just because you know who you are. I don't have a clue still. I'm split in two. You know where my other side is better than I do, and still you say I should just go along with everything. Feel the love, yeah? I'm done with all this niceness with humans. Margaret, what has she done for me?"

Nano piped up, "She has enabled you to be this rag of a spirit you call yourself. Margaret couldn't rely on you for guidance, remember? You sent her to the loony bin, remember? Yes, She Wolf, that was you that let her go. You could have stopped that."

The two wolves stood stalwartly, each in his or her own anger. Their fumes could be sensed in the room below, and people began to feel restless.

Margaret, too, felt a strange energy enter the room. For the first time in many years, she was deeply afraid. She tried to convince herself while talking to the audience. She tried to keep it back, and then she looked at them and could see that they, too, were feeling it.

Trudy had stood up and walked to the west side of the room; Hanna also stood and walked to the eastern side. Margaret could feel their protection like a rainbow bridge beaming across the room. She was standing in the south and looked directly to the back of the seats in the north and saw Nano there. She also saw Nala but barely recognized the mangled image she projected.

Mar continued her talk and came to the time where she opened the floor to questions from the audience. A woman in the back of the room stood up. Margaret recognized her immediately, but she didn't look like the beautiful young lady she'd been talking to these past few days. She'd aged fifty years, looked haggard, and was pale as ice. She was walking toward Margaret. Nano leaped toward her.

As Nano neared Nala's alter image, the woman, he could see her wolf image in shadow form behind the woman; her eyes were set on Margaret. Her ghostly gaze felt like a poisonous fog surrounding her.

Nala spoke silently to herself, but Nano could hear her. "See, see what I can do if I want!" she seethed. "I could turn this whole room into a swirling mess of wind and bodies if I liked, you know."

Nano ushered himself close to the woman and looked intensely at Nala's shadow-being. "You could. But can you tell me why first? What will you achieve?"

"I will destroy her life again! Isn't that what I'm supposed to do, Nano? Aren't I supposed to give her lessons? Well, here then, let me turn this room into chaos, and they will turn against her. They will think she brings in demons, and they will abandon her and she can go back to being crazy and learning the lessons. How do you like that, Nano?"

Nala used all of her energy fighting with Nano, and the woman dropped to the ground and lost all power and then disappeared.

Margaret nearly dropped over in shock when the woman disappeared, and she looked around at the audience to assess the damage. They hadn't noticed! They were still focused on her. She looked up to the back of the area and could see a shadow play on the partitions: two wolves were fighting it out, leaping at each other, jaws and teeth colliding, paws swiping as their hind legs dug into nothing and leaped into the heavens.

Hanna, Trudy, and Lynn were fully focused on Margaret. They created a protective shelter of golden light that surrounded her. Margaret could feel the protection and was able to continue her talk.

Chapter 11

Margaret looked down into the audience and toward Hanna and Trudy, who were holding the energy in the east and west directions of the room. She realized that Nano had abandoned his post in the north to brawl with Nala. She sent her spirit body to the north to hold the power of the great spirit in the room. As the northern winds blew through her, her voice took over, and the wolf song received its final verse.

> I call in the powers of the four directions;
> I call in the clouds of the seven chakras.
> I call in great spirit.
> I call in mother earth.
> I call in father sky and stars and moons above us.
>
> May my spirits unite.
> May I be whole and true.
> May my splits be mere wrinkles
> In this sea of life, and may my waves be calm and full
> As they renew with each time they hit the shore.
>
> My dear wolf spirit within,
> Come without the shadow that stalks you.
> Bring her in and love her as you would your own.
> Let her merge with you,
> Become you, as you become her,
> And yours will be mine and mine will be yours.

When she finished, she reopened the question and answer session, and a woman stood up in the crowd and spoke.

"Hello, thank you for your work. I am a mother of three, and one of my boys was in the Vietnam War. When he came home, he was not the same and spoke to us of 'demons' that had 'entered' him when he was in battle in the jungle. These 'demons' convinced him to end his life. I am looking for answers. Can you give me answers?"

She sat back down, bent over in tears.

Margaret climbed off the stage and went over to her. She held her tight and began to sing the chorus of the wolf song in her ear. "Oh, softly I touch... Let our spirits show."

The woman looked up at her and could feel a strong surge of energy swell in her heart. Her tears became joyful, and she felt a strength she had not felt before. Her inside spirit was awakening into a white bird; its wings stretched twelve feet across, and its dovetail fanned across the span. Her spirit was wild, yet contained. She stood on the woman's shoulder and let her wings fall to her sides, making her look angelic.

"There, there, beautiful soul, you are alive and here for a purpose, and you will find it with the help of your bird spirit. Do you know her?" Margaret asked the woman.

"I, I, I don't know, ma'am. I feel uplifted, as if I had wings—is that what you mean?"

"Yes, dear, and you feel your grief has slightly released itself from you?"

"I do! I do! I can think of Chris now and not feel my whole body convulse into grief. Thank you."

Margaret walked back to the stage area and sat down beside her altar. "Now then, any more questions?"

"I have one." That voice again. Margaret knew the shadow-being was back.

This time Nala appeared as a man. He was ancient, and he walked bent over, leaning on sticks that made a drumbeat rhythm as he came from the back of the room.

"Yes, sir, what is your question?"

"Can you teach me how I can kill you with sound?"

The room went silent; people shifted in their seats, and an uncomfortable feeling spread throughout the room.

Margaret could feel her neck begin to burn with fear and her temples pulsate. She took a deep breath and looked at him straight in the eye. She remembered one thing: a sorcerer can never kill you; he can only make you kill yourself. She glared at the man and said indignantly, "What kind of question is that? Do you want to use sound as a weapon, or do you actually want to kill me?"

"Both," he said solemnly and looked down at the floor.

Nano and Nala had both drawn blood and were caked in leaves, dust, and mud. Their exhausted selves were panting and grunting, still glaring, and each was ready to pounce again. They felt a being above them, and it distracted them from their brawl; its billowing wings felt heavy on their shoulders. The weight quieted them, and they surrendered themselves to the wind from the wings. Then the creature swooped into their view from above.

It was a phoenix. Its colors were magnificent hues of red, orange, yellow, and black, mostly black, and its raven-like wings sustained the creature's ability to hover in front of them in—now in clear view. Its squawk was difficult to follow, but they knew he was displeased. He flapped his wings at them in a scolding manner and let his displeasure be known. "You two, stop this at once! Wolf, go back to your other half, down there in the audience. Take your shadow back and be at peace with her, and the threat on Margaret will cease."

Nala stood up facing the phoenix. "I didn't send her away! It was him," she said, glaring at Nano. "He's the one who told me to send it all away and let her experience the lessons for me."

"Well, you didn't get it then, and you don't get it now," the phoenix said. "I am the symbol of transformation; I am the fire and the awakening. I can burn and destroy and reemerge in a new form."

The wolves listened intently to this powerful bird, and both of them set their attention to the old man, who was withering anyway. Nala pulled back her shadow-being from him, and he burst into flames, almost disappearing into a plume of violet smoke.

Margaret breathed a sigh of relief and again left her altar; she walked over to the old man. She knew that he was about to disappear, and she walked him out the door. The horrible things the man had said still lingered in her. He hadn't said much, but the word *kill* kept repeating itself in her brain.

She looked over at Hanna, who was in deep meditation back in the front row, as were Lynn and Trudy. Patrick was alert and smiled and gave her a discreet wave. She smiled back.

"Are there any more questions?" she asked meekly.

The room broke into applause, and Margaret could feel their gratitude and appreciation. She sat and basked in the love replenishing her from the attacks she'd endured.

She knew she had much work to do to bring peace to her animal spirit, Nala; she had neglected her, and she knew it. Deep regret came over her as she looked up to Nala. She, too, felt the vibration change created by the phoenix.

The applause sounded like a thousand winged ones. She closed her eyes and could see a chorus of songbirds serenading her wolf. Nano was there, together with an elk and a bear. She felt the warmth of the circle that Trudy, Lynn, and Hanna had created around her. She wanted to stay there, but she knew she had walk out of it now that the threat was gone. She knew somehow that they were working something out up there, and they would have a ceremony tonight when they got back to the hotel.

Walking off the stage, waving at everyone and then joining her sisters, was a journey for her as she witnessed where she was and where she came from and how it all fit together now. She could look easily into the future today and see a clear and well-lit path ahead; finally she was facing her shadow with love in her heart. Finally, she had the strength to look.

As the people got up and stretched and slowly filed out of the room, the animal spirits filled the room. Hanna, Trudy, and Lynn sat around the altar and brought up chairs for each spirit animal. Then Trudy changed her mind and asked Margaret to set up the altar on the floor and to make room for everyone to sit around it.

There was tension in the air. Everyone was reflecting, and no one but the wolves was really sure what had just occurred.

Once they were all breathing more easily, Lynn pulled out a stick from her bag; it was adorned with multicolored threads and paint. Crystals hung from its mini branches on threads entwined with shiny strings, and a few bells hung from the top. A long eagle feather just under the length of the stick hung down its side. Lynn picked it up and waved it a bit, and the eagle feather took flight; it caused a stream of sparkly fairy dust to follow. Heads turned and everyone's eyes were glued to the stick. Lynn held the stick straight before her. She touched her forehead with it and then kissed the stick softly.

She said, "Dear friends, I am grateful to be here in this circle of power; thank you for receiving me. I offer us an ancient native shamanic tool that has been used by many cultures around our mother earth. It is a talking stick, and it symbolizes the gateway of communication. It assures truth, and its holder is its only speaker. We all have a point of view, and we all have traveled a different journey this evening. We all have different stories to tell. As I pass this sacred talking stick to my right, our circle will be silent until the holder finishes and passes the stick on."

Trudy felt warm and true inside as she listened to Lynn. She hadn't spoken about this tool at home, and her girls were receiving a good teaching. She was grateful and gave Lynn a warm stroke on her shoulder as she received the talking stick from her.

"From my heart to your heart," Lynn said with tears in her eyes.

"It was a long time ago; many, many lives have passed. I was living in Wales," Trudy said, looking at Hanna and nodding acknowledgment of her constant questioning about her past life in Wales. "I was a young maiden, and we lived in the cottage where you lived, Hanna."

Hanna looked up, her mouth open, and was about to talk when she saw the talking stick and slowly closed her mouth.

"Yes, Hanna, I lived in that magical house as well. But it was a different time, a hostile period in history, when conditioning was an essential part of survival. People were not awarded for standing out at the time; rather, they lost their heads. And today, Hanna, you saw Wales from another point of view. It was in Wales that I went through periods of friction between my ego and brain, and my first attention being and my spiritual selves. I, too, gave away parts of myself that I did not like, and they came back to haunt me. But in every life, the lessons are different, which is what makes each journey so special. Do you remember Rupert in Wales? Do you remember his last words to me at the ball? Do you recall those words of liberation, of freedom, a completed cycle that has spanned many lifetimes, dear ones?"

She looked around the circle and focused very clearly on Nala, who squirmed at her glare. She squealed a howl and did her little dance of defiance.

"Wolf, you are Nala. You watched, you saw, and you heard Rupert give me my freedom, not that I hadn't already taken it. The taking of my power occurred back then that we speak of, in another lifetime, on familiar ground in Wales. I took off and left Rupert at the altar. I could not marry him then or now. And this was not what my spirit elk had intended. She was such a family beast. She yearned for a nest and a mate; she yearned in her womb for offspring, and it was the journey she had chosen. I had other plans and callings. I spent many lifetimes making this up, and the circle was completed in Wales with you, my family."

Trudy was weeping with joy. Hanna noticed her face was more creased than before and wondered how old she was. Her attention drew Trudy toward her, and they embraced.

Then Trudy turned to Margaret. "Margaret, it does not surprise me that you let your wolf go lazy. Nala was on a journey that did not serve you. You are fortunate and have many other allies in your life. You survived a big battle, and you will receive this part of your spirit back when you can. I pray for gratitude to heal and merge your spirit, and I will work to guide you on the road of self-forgiveness."

Trudy then sat in silence with her eyes closed and a glorious smile on her face. She held the talking stick tight in her hands, and after a few moments, she leaned forward, kissed it, and passed it to her elk spirit, who lay beside her.

Elk was normally silent. She tended to witness and provide stability through her nurturing being but never said much. Trudy had laid the stick in front of her in clear view. She was studying it and shuffled one hoof in the ground, bringing up some dust. Her breath became visible in the dust, and a voice emerged. "Ahhhhhh, yaaaaaay, yaaah, ahem… long time this fight. I saw this fight before, you wolves. There is a part of you who live beneath the sea; it is not their home. Bring them back to you. Make them clean, I say, make them clean. They hold a dark shadow, not yours. It gives you false power. You know false power? False power lives in your brain. It lives with a shadow, and its voice is your ego's motive, not your spirit's intent. Be careful, mmmmmmmMar, be careful," he said.

Nala rolled on her back and hung her legs in the air. She was pushing up quite a dust cloud, her exact intent, leaving her behind a veil, which no one wished to pass. Her circle's enduring trust was making her thoughts chaotic; her impulses were still manic, even though she kept herself under control. Her spirit neighbors knew her thoughts, and she knew theirs. Elk's energy spread through her with his words. They were comforting, yet they left her feeling helpless. She knew not how to reach the sea, let alone find part of her spirit.

Nano knew and got up to take the talking stick from Elk. He moved over to Nala and lay down next to her, leaving his hind leg to dangle over her belly. This left her stuck on her back without a wrestle with Nano. She submitted and listened to him as he slowly told her the story of sending her spirit to the sea.

"There was nothing else I could do with it; you just left it and ran off!" he protested as he realized the consequences of that night so long ago. "That was part of Margaret's path; she lived without you as a full spirit guide for all those years. Nala, it is time for you to be whole; it is time for you to come back. Are you clear? I will bring you the shadow. I will work with you and your shadow, but only you can heal it and only you will know the parts that are yours and the parts that are another's. You will leave those parts behind in the sea. We are all parts of light and dark, but you only have to own your own shadow. I will help you detach from the part that is not yours."

Nala turned over and licked Nano from head to toe; she nuzzled her nose in his ears and cleared them down to his butt, where she concentrated for a long time. The others turned away. Nala was ready to take the talking stick.

"And what part is that, Nano? Is it the part that loathes Margaret? Is it the part that only wants her dead?"

Everyone was put on alert when Nala began to come apart. They set their intent on shelter for her, and ensured that the channels to her heart would keep receiving light from them for balance as she struggled.

Nano took the talking stick from her for a moment. "Nala, my friend and maybe my mate someday… why don't we just ask it?"

Nano whispered something in Hanna's ear, and she got up from the circle and left the room. She returned with a large prayer stick from the stall they had set up. Hanna gave it to Nala, who held it gently in her mouth and sniffed it, pawing it, dropping it, and then picking it up again.

Nano continued. He picked up the prayer stick and stuck it in the ground so that it stood straight in front of the She Wolf's nose.

"Okay, Nala, look, that's your shadow. You see just an ordinary stick with some stuff on it; it can symbolize anything. Right now, it's your shadow. Talk to it."

Nala sniffled a bit. She let in a sigh that sounded like the inside of a lion's roar; they weren't sure if she was about to pounce or was kicking back in surrender.

"Why do you hate Margaret?" She was straightforward about it, no messing around.

Nala pawed around the planted stick. She could hear it roar from afar; it seemed so distant, as if it were on a midnight train on the way to nowhere. She listened some more. The sound seemed to become lighter and lighter until she heard nothing. Then the stick began to speak for the entire circle to hear.

"I am Nala; I am Margaret. I am the split that happened when. I see you from two branches always: in the heart of me, I am in love; but in the head of me, I hate, I loathe, I seethe. I ask for balance, which I don't know. I ask for an unknown to make me one again. Do you know where it is?"

Nala and Margaret were plopped next to each other. Each word they heard felt like a dagger in their hearts. As the stick talked about its split and the females felt it, the energies slowly began to mix. The stick received compassion, and the hearts received reason and intent. There was no agreement, forgiveness, or deals—only a new known concept, that in their oneness they would find the wholeness… that we are all one; it was all that made sense.

Patrick sat up and looked intently at the talking stick, which was lying in the middle of the circle next to the prayer stick, Margaret, and Nala. Mar nodded at him, and he reached over and took it. Patrick could only feel the spirit animals—he could not see them—and Hanna wasn't sure if that was up to the wolves or him. He did accept their existence, and he communicated with Nano often. He just couldn't see them.

Patrick sat down next to the prayer stick with the beautifully painted talking stick in his hand. "You speak of this split," he addressed the shadow. "Tell me more about that. You paint it as branches from a tree, and that tells me that you speak of one source." He laid the talking stick next to the shadow, still held within the prayer stick, and waited.

"I am one, and I am two; I am all three. There is no glue that holds me together; every idea or notion creates another one. You see? It's a matter of survival," the shadow bellowed.

Patrick took the talking stick and examined it. He found a spot in the center of the stick and blew gently into it. "I send you love and acceptance from the heart of this bridge of communication between all of our selves to you and your voice of one."

Suddenly the prayer stick fell over on the ground. At the same time, Nala jumped up in the air with the flight of a puppy and yelped out a few childish squeals. Everyone looked at the prayer stick. Lynn picked it up carefully and wrapped it in red cloth. She walked to the partition door and put it outside on a chair.

As she walked back in, her eyes were on the talking stick. "Patrick, you have some touch! I'm very impressed with the gateway you provided. How did you know that love would heal this serpent we saw?" she asked.

"I have never seen anything that hasn't healed with love, Lynn. I only wish I could practice it. You know, in my profession, this is a classic case of schizophrenia. Our methods, although drastically advanced from the sixties and seventies, are still primitive. There is a difference between primitive methods and ancient methods... I am learning to blend the two to the extent that my system will allow."

Hanna lit some sage and walked around the area, cleansing it, clearing herself, blowing away the cobwebs that collected drama, and feeling clear paths ahead.

It was getting late, and the expo was closing up. The group needed to disperse but were not yet ready to. Margaret put away the altar; she wrapped up all of the crystals and rolled up the cloth. Then they walked over to the hotel, and after checking in and freshening up, they gathered in Trudy's room. Room service was ordered for a late dinner; they were all famished and thirsty and needed food.

Once they were fed and satisfied, they felt grounded. Hanna and Patrick cuddled on the sofa, and Margaret was on the floor with Trudy. Lynn seemed preoccupied, and the phoenix sat on the back of the sofa above Hanna. He kept pecking at her head gently, and she would wave it away with her hand unconsciously, totally ignorant of who this bird represented in their circle. He stuck to her like glue. The wolves sat in front of the fireplace and dozed.

Hanna got up and took the talking stick. She walked back to the sofa and sat with it for a while. She ran her finger up and down the stick and searched for its heart; then she realized that her other hand was covering it. She was holding onto the heart of the talking stick and released her grip slightly. She knew that she had much to say and began to assemble her thoughts with the flow she felt from the heart of this magical talking stick. Everyone focused on her as her first voice came out.

"I feel great relief and thanks today. When I sit with you, my sisters, and Patrick, my lover, I am full. I was prepared this evening as the wolves visited me on my way over here on the plane. This shadow, that I remember; and I remember it well. That day when we were kids and Margaret, your wolf, she just didn't know who she was. She wasn't bad or anything; she just felt separate and different and alien, and we didn't know what to do with her, so yes, I remember, we did send her away. And now we know what happens when you do that. You can't just send it away when it is part of you. You have to heal it; otherwise it will fester and move into the shadows.

"In school, I study old things and past civilizations on this earth. I witness the religions they followed from their sacred objects. I dig them up out of the ground. In the same way, we dig our own shadows up from down under, and it's similar. If what we dig up is in bad condition, we restore it with cleansings and repair it just like we would dig up a shadow-being from our spirit. We cleanse it and nurture it before we merge with it. This lesson is so important.

"I sit here with my lover, Patrick, who feels us and also has medical education; it brings me joy that he can feed from this experience. He witnesses mental illness every day, and tonight he witnessed spiritual dis-ease and the easing of the spirit. I am grateful and want to gift you with some wonderful news."

Hanna sat back on the sofa into Patrick's arms, with the talking stick lying across her lap. She grinned toward him, and he smiled into her eyes. The love was felt by everyone, and the wolves let out a short soprano-pitched howl. which sounded like *Ho*!

Hanna continued, "Patrick and I have decided to make a baby! I know. We have to find a place to live first and decide if I'm coming back to the States and all that, but we wanted you to know that we are planning a family somewhere."

Hanna looked over at Margaret, who was crying happy tears, and got up to hug her. Margaret held her tight, and Hanna felt her body cry and release; she knew Margaret was overjoyed but overwhelmed right now. She whispered in her ear, "Oh softly we touch, Oh softly we know, and it is now we show, dear sister. I love you so."

A beeping sound interrupted Hanna and Margaret. Patrick dug into his pocket, pulled out his beeper, and pressed a button. "I have to call the office; they only call if it's an emergency," he said as he got up in search of the telephone.

"I think it's my dad," Hanna said. "I wish he were here."

Patrick came back into the sitting area and said, "Ask and you shall receive, my love!" He had the telephone in his hand and was holding the receiver in the other. "Here he is," he said and handed the phone to Hanna.

"Hanny? Is that you?" Jay asked.

Hanna tried to visualize her dad in her head and closed her eyes, saying nothing.

"Hanna? Are you there?" he asked again.

"Um, yeah, Dad." She could feel her little girl voice inside; her face flushed, and her mouth went dry. She reached for a drink and handed the talking stick to her dad in her vision. "Oh Dad, you have the floor; talk!" she announced to him and held the phone's receiver in the air so everyone could hear him. His voice carried well, and they listened intently.

"Um, well, hello. I wasn't prepared for a broadcast," he murmured. "I was going to talk to my daughter, but if you all want to listen, may you all be witnesses."

Hanna could feel Jay's lawyer voice drift in, and her body shuddered. "Dad, we can speak privately, if you like, if it makes you feel uncomfortable."

Jay was surprised at Hanna's empathy and assured by her. "Yes, let's speak privately. I have something to tell you; you can talk about it with your friends later. But first I want to congratulate Margaret on her first event in New York! That's a big accomplishment; you should be proud," he said and added, "that is, if you are all allowed to be proud."

"Of course we are, Dad! It's not like we are allowed or not allowed to do anything; more like there are no rules to our paths but a commitment to our truth. I know that would sound ambiguous to a lawyer, so look at it from an artist point of view. See that in the creativity of our lives and our sense of gratitude and connection to the land and the stars, we are not drawn to anything but our truth. It's a commitment and a self-responsibility that we practice. So you see, when you look at it from a creative perspective, you can see that Margaret has much to be proud of, and you are, aren't you, Mar?"

Margaret nodded and smiled. "Tell your dad thank you."

Hanna shimmied over to the other side of the sofa and stretched out her legs toward Patrick; he began to massage her feet, and she lay her head back on the cushy sofa arm. "Yeah, Dad, Mar says thank you. So tell me, what's so urgent tonight to you that you call? I can't wait to hear you!" Hanna said warmly and thankfully.

"My daughter, I have so much to tell you. My thoughts have fallen into place in my head, and I am beginning to feel my soul again and my heartbeat. For so many years, I was a dead spirit inside a needy ego, and I resented it. From my law school days, when I was first learning the stuff, I could feel that it was going to turn me into a different person, and I accepted it and transformed into an asshole. I was so far deep into it that I could not see myself from another's perspective and became controlling in order to maintain my masquerade. I could train the world to fear me, but I couldn't qualm my own fears.

"Hanna, none of this will ever begin to justify what I did on that dark night when I destroyed our lives and ended your mother's and Mikey's. Nothing. I can only tell it as it was, and it was not 'the me' I have found within myself in recent years.

"Hanna, what happened tonight at the expo? I felt something of concern this evening, and that is also why I called. Something inside spoke to me; it felt like a bird, though I've only heard of these things from you. Yes, I felt like there was a big bird inside, and I could feel the wings and feel his motion. It was a transformation, and it changed me this evening. I became very present. Do you understand?"

Hanna thought of the phoenix that had appeared this evening and how she'd wondered who it belonged to. "Dad?"

"Yeah, doll?"

"Did the bird you felt inside you appear like a phoenix?"

"Well, it may have been, but it began as a small bird, gray in color, and its feathers were puffed out, making him appear larger. But then he changed into all shapes and sizes, just a big mix of movement. I could feel these moves like they were changes occurring within my spirit. And as the bird became more present with me, it burst into flames and turned into dust."

"Dad, you are beginning to attune with us in spirit; I believe the phoenix represents you in the spirit plane. He was very helpful to us tonight; in fact, he saved us. Did you know? Dad, I am grateful to you."

"No, Hanna, I can only be grateful to you, for you still speak with me. I do not deserve your gratitude."

"It doesn't matter if you deserve it or not, Dad. I deserve it. I forgave you a long time ago. For me. Dad, I have had a great life as a result of your actions. I could have remained stuck in anger at you and grief for my mother and my brother. I could have lived my whole life within that grief and with all of the guilt that I was the survivor. Yes, I could have, but I did not and I will not. I can be modest and polite and say that I made the best of a very bad situation, or I can stand up and say thank you; my life is blessed thanks to you, Dad. In retrospect, we would have battled each other about my friendship with Trudy; you might have banned me from her, who knows? The *why's* are the mystery, Dad, and I don't look for those answers anymore. I trust."

"Hanna, you have grown up to be a very wise woman, and I respect you so. You are my daughter, but I cannot take credit for your beauty. It shines beyond my dreams as we reconstruct our relationship. I congratulate you on your union with Patrick..."

"Oh, Dad, I forgot to tell you; we are planning a grandchild for you!"

The hairs on Jay's arms rose as he heard Hanna's announcement. His face flushed, and he tried to speak. "That's..." and he hiccupped a sob. "Hanny... darling, I love you." It was all he managed before he fell to his knees and prayed to God. He cried and moaned and cried again, "Rejoice, rejoice, rejoice." One of the nurses heard him and came running to his room only to find Jay in great shape, dancing in celebration, but making a racket.

"Dad, are you there?" Hanna listened to him celebrate. Her heart warmed, and she told him good night.

Margaret came over, gave Hanna a hug, and said, "See, Hanna, we've all faced our shadows tonight. We have acted with grace and with honor. Thank you for coming all this way. You must be exhausted."

Hanna looked at her watch; it was past midnight, and she realized she'd been awake over twenty-four hours. Sleep was calling her.

Patrick moved closer and hugged her close; she rested her head on his shoulder and closed her eyes.

Everyone else closed their eyes for a moment; Lynn bent over and took the talking stick.

"I have spent but a few hours with you tonight, and you feel like family already. Thank you for your reception and warmness. We have witnessed several battles here tonight and have emerged inspired, joyful, and transformed. Even the phoenix could not resist working with us tonight and traveled many miles, leaving Jay on his own, to assist in the last stand for your alter-ego spirit, Nala. I am grateful for the teaching I received today, watching the way you held yourself, Mar, when you were being attacked. Thank you; it gave me courage, and it could have made me fearful."

Lynn looked over at Trudy, who was sitting next to her on the floor. "My dear friend of many lifetimes! It is an honor always to hear your prayers. Trudy, so goodenough, elk woman of the north, you hold this stature dearly and sacredly, and we are grateful to you. You have raised these girls as your own, and they have grown to be women of power, honoring their paths of heart while remaining in circle over long periods of absence. It takes true power to hold a circle so remote and infrequent. I see it structured divinely by the wolves; each decade of absence imposed, but providing long gaps to grow into and expand. You are truly magical!"

Trudy bowed her head, and took Lynn's hands and raised them to hear forehead and then to her heart. Trudy was weeping silently; her calm smile shone, as did her eyes. She beamed with pride as Mar and Hanna joined them and they all embraced. Nano and Nala stood together above them in the heavens and sang their song to the moon as Patrick and Jay's phoenix stood silently witnessing.

When they finally found their beds, a sacred celestial harmony with a chorus of angels lullabied them to sleep. It was the kind of scene the angels speak of and it held love for which there are no words.

"Beautiful ending, Lisa. Great spiritual fight and wonderful healing!"
Nancy Gannon, Sister in Circle

Made in the USA
San Bernardino, CA
28 November 2013